From Dawn to Dusk

*Memoirs of an
Amish/Mennonite Farm Boy*

By
Will Troyer

Llumina Press

Copyright 2003 Will Troyer

All rights reserved. No part of this publication may be reproduced or transmitted in any form or by any means electronic or mechanical, including photocopy, recording, or any information storage and retrieval system, without permission in writing from both the copyright owner and the publisher.

Requests for permission to make copies of any part of this work should be mailed to Permissions Department, Llumina Press, PO Box 772246, Coral Springs, FL 33077-2246

ISBN: 1-932303-54-5
Printed in the United States of America

*To my siblings Almeda, Joel, Sylvia, Miriam, Omar, and Philip
who shared the rural farm life with me.*

ACKNOWLEDGMENTS

I owe a great deal of thanks to my family and many friends who encouraged me to record some of the memories of my rural boyhood.

I'm grateful to my son Eric who critiqued each chapter as the manuscript progressed and made many suggestions as to the contents and organization of the book. I'm especially thankful to my wife LuRue who patiently edited the punctuation and grammar while retaining the colloquialisms of my upbringing. The book would not have been completed without her constantly shepherding it to publication form.

CONTENTS

Preface

1.	Roots	1
2.	Chores	7
3.	Horse Power	13
4.	The Neighborhood	19
5.	Going to Preaching	27
6.	Lattweich Time	33
7.	Food Aplenty	37
8.	The Depression	43
9.	We Become Mennonites	47
10.	Dad Buys a Car	53
11.	We Move	59
12.	A New School	63
13.	Beauty the Pony	71
14.	Dad Buys a Tractor	79
15.	The Blizzard of '36	85
16.	Livestock and Pets	91
17.	Electricity Comes to Our House	97
18.	Old Ben	103
19.	The Hartman Place	109
20.	Spring on the Farm	115
21.	Haymaking	121
22.	The Swimmin' Hole	127
23.	Threshing Time	133
24.	The Fall Harvest	141
25.	Halloweening	147
26.	The Wildlife Harvest	153
27.	A Clash of Generations	159
28.	Bicycle West	165
29.	Farewell to the Farm	175

PREFACE

I come from a long line of Amish farmers. The Amish, sometimes known as the "Plain People," have lived their segregated lifestyles for several hundred years and firmly cling to their beliefs and customs to this day. They resist changes that might force them into the modern world.

Even though the Amish wish to live alone without attracting attention from outsiders, they stand out like a flashing beacon with their old-fashioned clothes and simple ways, and their use of horses and buggies for transportation.

You'll know you've entered an Amish rural community by the simple manicured white houses, clean barns, and neatly kept fields. If it is summertime, you'll see men and boys working the fields with horse-drawn equipment, dressed in plain-colored clothes and broad-brimmed hats. Here and there you'll see a horse and buggy traveling down a country road driven by an Amish woman wearing a dress of a solid color and a large black bonnet. She is accompanied by several small children dressed in similar fashion.

Where did these Amish come from, and what are some of their beliefs?

The Amish are direct descendants of the Swiss Anabaptists who split from the Roman Catholic Church in Europe about 1525, during the Reformation. They believed the Church had become too legalistic and authoritative, the leaders being more interested in political power than in following the teachings of the Bible. The Anabaptists gained their name because they did not believe in the infant baptism practiced by the Catholic Church. They also believed in the separation of church and state. Their disagreements with the Roman Catholic Church caused many Anabaptists to be jailed or killed. A popular way to eliminate these religious reformers was to burn them at the stake or drown them by holding the victims underwater in a net. Such measures did not stop the movement, however, as it spread throughout much of central Europe from Switzerland to Holland.

Many religious sects developed during this period. Among them were the Swiss Mennonites, who did not believe in participating in wars or violence. They reverted to a more primitive, simpler type of life practiced by the early Christians. They were relentlessly persecuted for their beliefs, so many of them migrated to northern Germany, Prussia, Russia, and later to the United States. To avoid persecution, they often settled in mountain hinterlands and thus became expert tillers of the less productive soils in order to survive.

The Amish emerged as a division of the Swiss Mennonites about 1700 and were the followers of Jakob Ammann. He believed the Mennonites, after several generations, had become too lax in their religious rules, which included manner of dress. He instigated strict discipline: the wearing of simple clothing and beards for men but not the mustaches that were then in fashion for the well-dressed man in Europe. Hooks and eyes were used on coats in place of buttons to distinguish the Amish from the military men with large bright buttons on their uniforms.

He also instigated the rule of *shunning*. Any member who broke the rules was banned from the church. Members in good standing could not eat or associate with banned members until they publicly confessed their sins and were reunited with the church. Sometimes this meant separating husband and wife. Shunning is still practiced today by the Amish as a means of keeping their members in line, an experience my family encountered after leaving the Amish church.

Early groups of Amish emigrated to the British Colonies in North America between 1737 and 1754. William Penn, a Quaker, encouraged them to settle in Pennsylvania because they were pious people and good farmers. Another wave of Amish emigrated in the early- to mid-19th century. Today, no Amish remain in Europe. Most live in North America, concentrated around Lancaster, Pennsylvania; Holmes County, Ohio; and northern Indiana. Smaller groups are found in Midwestern states such as Iowa, Missouri, Illinois, Michigan, Kentucky, Minnesota, and Kansas, as well as in the states of New York, Delaware, Maryland, Florida, Montana, and in the province of Ontario in Canada. The total population is around 150,000.

The Amish have their own language, called Pennsylvania Dutch (Dutch being from Deutsch, the German word for German). The language is a dialect of High German, which is still spoken in the Rhineland area of Germany, with a smattering of English and other colloquial phrases. It's the language spoken at home and the first language I learned as a lad. However, nearly all Amish are also fluent in English, which the children learn when they enter school.

The modest dress of the Amish is similar to that worn by the 16th-century Europeans. Men wear black broad-brimmed hats and black suits with straight collars. Hooks and eyes fasten coats instead of buttons, and broad suspenders support the pants instead of belts. In place of a zippered fly, a broad flap held up by buttons can be dropped. Work clothing is usually plain denim material, all sewn by the women. Men use straw hats in the summer. All married men wear beards and hair long enough to cover much of their ears. Mustaches are verboten.

Women wear dark solid-colored dresses usually in lavender, green, blue, gray, or black, with the hem well below the knees. They also wear a cape, a thin fabric which fits over the shoulder in a triangular shape; when outside, they wear a warm shawl. Church rules forbid women to cut their hair, so they put it up into braids without ribbons or they fasten it into a roll on the backs of their heads. They cover their heads with a white prayer cap. The finely pleated caps take a lot of time and skill to sew. The women use a large black bonnet over the prayer cap when traveling or going to church. Children's clothes mimic the adults in color and form.

Much of how the Amish differ from the modern world is based on strict Biblical interpretation of Romans 12:1, "Be not conformed to this world...." To the Amish this means one should not dress and behave like the rest of the world.

Variations in the rules can dictate Amish life a bit from one church district to another, but basically all adhere to a simple lifestyle with no electricity, TV, radio, telephones, central heating system, or automobiles. The Amish use horses for farming and can employ tractors only for work that cannot be accomplished with horses, such as powering a belt that drives a grain-threshing machine. They do not believe in getting a formal education beyond the eighth grade. They fear a high school atmosphere during the crucial teenage years will tempt their children to leave the Amish ways for the modern world. This practice has been a bone of contention in many states where laws dictate that all children must attend school through age sixteen. Amish parents sometimes sat in jail for refusing to send their children to modern high schools until the United States Supreme Court ruled in their favor in 1972. Many Amish communities now have their own schools. In addition they will not accept government handouts, such as agriculture crop supports or Social Security.

The bishop of each church district enforces all rules and regulations. Members who fail to follow the guidelines are warned and if they do not comply, they are excommunicated and shunned.

My family and I experienced security in being part of such a community, for the Amish take care of one another. They do not believe in insurance, but if a member loses a house or a barn, the whole community pitches in to replace the loss. Most Amish people believe that adhering to the old ways, keeping close family ties, and upholding religious beliefs are far more important than the conveniences of modern technology. A few discontented Amish leave the church, usually because they are tempted by modern conveniences, such as automobiles, to ease their rigid lifestyle. This is especially true among the young people, and today approximately 20 percent of the children leave the Amish Society.

I

ROOTS

The eight-year-old Amish boy struggled to keep the one-row cultivator shovels astride the row of corn. The team of Belgian horses knew the routine and never faltered. The boy's wide-brimmed straw hat, denim pants, and short-sleeved shirt were the only protection he had against the relentless sun. The horses plodded to the end of the field, then stopped when the boy yelled "Whoa!" and pulled on the lines.

He stood up, grabbed the large steel handle on his right with both hands, and pulled down, lifting the cultivator shovels off the ground. Then he turned to his left and repeated the process on the other half of the cultivator. "Giddyup! Haw!" he directed the team and pulled on the left line.

As the horses slowly swung left, the boy guided the team forward a few steps before lining them up with another row of corn. He stopped the horses, reached up, and released the handle on each side, dropping the cultivator shovels to the ground.

The horses were hot and sweaty so he decided to rest them for a few minutes. He climbed off the cultivator, walked to the fencerow, and pulled up several handfuls of succulent green grass; he offered each of the Belgians a mouthful of the greens. He was building a rapport with the horses, just as his dad had taught him.

After a few minutes, he climbed back on the cultivator and said "Giddyup." The team responded and the shovels sliced off the young weeds that had started growing in the cornfield. A few flies buzzed around the horses and they switched their tails constantly to discourage the pests from landing. Occasionally the Belgians shook their heads and snuffled when the flies tried to land on their heads and necks.

Halfway down the field a large horsefly zoomed around the team, making them nervous and uneasy. Quickly the boy stopped the team, jumped from the cultivator and moved along the side of one of the horses. When the large fly landed, he swatted it with his hat. The stunned fly fell to the ground, and the boy stomped it into the dirt with his bare foot. "*Du bist dote*! (You are dead!)" he said to the dead fly with some satisfaction.

All day the farm boy continued driving the horses down the rows of corn, occasionally giving them a rest. It was slow, tedious work; it was also part of his expected duties.

It's hard to believe now, but I was that Amish boy.

I was born in 1925 of Old Order Amish parents on a farm near McGrawsville, Indiana. I was expected to follow in the footsteps of my ancestors—to be part of the Amish Society and to pass on our plain traditions and religious beliefs to my children as each generation had done for centuries. But most of all, I was expected to become a farmer, for the Amish are closely tied to the soil. On farms within close-knit communities they are able to meet their simple needs of food, clothing, shelter and to live their religious convictions relatively free from the modern world that surrounds them.

My ancestors were direct descendants of the Anabaptist movement in medieval Europe and Amish from their beginnings in 1693. My great-great-grandfather Marner on my mother's side lived in Bern, Switzerland, and had hired out as a stable boy in Napoleon's army. He died during the retreat from Moscow, leaving a young wife of nineteen years and a small son Jacob Marner, born in 1798. The widow did not want her son to become involved in the frequent wars in Europe, so they emigrated to the United States around 1815.

Another ancestor on my mother's side, John Smucker, was born near Grindelvald, Switzerland, in 1789; he emigrated to the United States in the early 1800s. He reached Miami County, Indiana, from Holmes County, Ohio, in 1850. He was one of the first Amishmen to go to that county after it was opened for settlement.

My father's ancestors were some of the early immigrants to the American Colonies, arriving prior to 1750. My grandfather Joel Troyer arrived in Miami County, Indiana, from Holmes County, Ohio, in 1901. He had a large family of eight children. My father Martin Troyer, the youngest and a twin, was born in 1896.

He and my mother Katy Marner, born in 1901, were married in

1920 and settled on a seventy-eight-acre farm my father had purchased just before their marriage. The farm was in the middle of a 640-acre section of land, accessed by a half-mile-long lane. It was a typical Amish farm with a large two-story barn. The ground floor provided room for horses, cows, some grain bins, and a few implements. The large mow above was filled with hay and straw. Completing the complex were a plain white house with a nearby summer kitchen and numerous outbuildings such as a chicken house, a pig shed, and a combination granary and implement shed. An outdoor toilet stood near the house. It was a three-holer, two large ones for adults and a small one in the middle for kids. The Sears Roebuck catalogs that lay on the seats sufficed as toilet paper.

Like most Midwest farms of that era, ours was run as a general farm with a variety of livestock and crops. My parents had cows, pigs, draft horses for working the fields, and one or two lighter horses for pulling the buggy. A flock of sheep kept down the weeds, and several hundred chickens provided eggs and meat for both home use and sale. Basic crops were corn, wheat, oats, soybeans, and hay. We fed the corn, oats, and hay to the livestock and sold most of the soybeans and wheat as cash crops. We rotated the crops to maximize the nutrients in the soil and spread livestock manure on the fields to enrich them. Today these farming practices are called organic farming.

A huge garden supplied many vegetables; almost everything the family ate was produced on the farm. A small orchard yielded peaches, pears, plums, cherries, and an abundance of apples for canning and making cider and apple butter. A small woods on the farm provided fuel for the stoves and some pasture for the cows.

I was the third of seven children. As was typical of those days, my mother gave birth to all her children at home. Dr. Kratzer, a rural family doctor who worked out of nearby Wawpecong, delivered me. My mother told me that I weighed 9½ pounds at birth. One of her friends said, "He doesn't look Amish." The statement rather upset my mother; perhaps it was an omen.

Though my family was Old Order Amish in my early youth, in many ways our life did not differ greatly from the farm life of our non-Amish neighbors. In general, farming was still a family enterprise in which young children were expected to participate. Tractors and other technological advancements were just beginning to show up on family farms; they would alter forever the social life of many of the agricultural people who had thrived without them for many generations.

I'm sure no one anticipated the rapid changes that would occur after World War II. Everything became mechanized. With a large tractor, a plow, a combine, and other equipment, a farmer with one hired hand could easily farm three to four hundred acres. This was a far cry from the 60 to 160 acres that required the efforts of a large family in my early youth. Horses were no longer needed and were being phased out of the equation. Many farmers began to specialize in farming grain, or in raising cattle or hogs. Thus the general farms of the '20s, '30s, and '40s, with their mix of livestock and grain farming, became a thing of the past. On many farms, children, like their counterparts in the city, were left with few chores and were no longer active participants in the everyday farm work previous generations had experienced.

As fewer farmers were needed to till the soil, more people moved to the cities to work in the factories that now produced the numerous handy gadgets everyone desired. It was the beginning of a huge social disruption that is still going on today. Many of the former farmers and other city residents were unable to cope with these rapid changes, contributing to an increase in the rate of crime, drug, and alcohol use. As I look back, I can deeply appreciate the simple joys we experienced from hard work and close social contact with our families and neighbors. They ingrained in my siblings and me a strong work ethic, and instilled in us a respect for our fellow beings.

The Amish are one of the few groups that are still trying to cling to the old ways. Even they have problems resisting change; many of their children are tempted by the modern world and often succumb to life in the fast lane. As you will see, I too left the uncomplicated lifestyle, as did most of my family in one form or another. I hope, however, that the Amish will continue to live their old ways. We have much to learn from their efforts to live close to the earth and to God.

*My father and mother, Martin and Katie Troyer,
after they retired from farming*

2

CHORES

On the farm everyone participated in the many tasks. The work assigned to each member of the family depended upon age, physical ability, and gender. The Amish are known for their strong work ethic; hard work is next to godliness in their eyes. As small children we were always eager to help and were praised by our parents for our efforts. "*Er shaft goot*," "He works real good." "Look at his little hands and feet go. He is a good worker," I would hear my mother remark, which spurred my efforts. Of course, once the task became routine and perhaps a little boring, comments from my mother and father were more likely to be, "*Dobba, dobba!*"("Hurry, hurry!"). "You haven't got all day."

As we advanced in age and ability, our parents assigned us greater responsibilities and more jobs. As a rule we took each new assignment eagerly, for we wanted to help and to be ever more useful members of the family. Advancing from one job to another was a natural way of growing to adulthood.

One of the first duties of small children on our farm was to keep the bins behind the kitchen stove filled with wood and corncobs. The cobs were a cheap by-product of the corn crop and, doused with a little kerosene, were a quick source of heat. Mother would add wood to sustain the fire in the old cast-iron cooking range. Children were given this job at four years of age or even younger. With little buckets, we made several trips to fill the bins. As we got older and stronger the job became easier.

Small kids also filled the teakettle and the warm water reservoir on the end of the stove. We didn't have running water but instead hauled water from the pump house. Drying dishes was an early chore and, as soon as we were tall enough to stand on a box and get our elbows above the sink and dishpan, we helped wash the dirty dishes. As we boys became older and were assigned more barn duties, dishwashing became a job primarily for the girls.

We performed morning chores on a tight schedule. When we reached school age, our chores had to be completed and breakfast eaten in time to catch the school bus. That meant getting up about 5:30 A.M. and dressing quickly. Dad and the boys headed for the barn while Mom and the girls got the stove going, breakfast started, and lunch pails packed.

Dad usually took care of the hogs while my older brother Joel and I pitched down hay, fed the horses, and filled each cow manger with the allotted feed. We then chased the cows in from the barn lot and fastened them into the stanchions, which held them in place for milking. Milking was a major task on our farm and everyone helped.

I first started milking when I was five. Many times I had watched my parents and older sister Almeda squeeze the teats to make the milk flow. One morning I asked Mom if I could try. It looked simple, but I had to learn to close off the top of the teat near the udder with my thumb and forefinger, then squeeze the trapped milk from the teat with the other three fingers. It's the same system a calf uses while suckling. My hands were small, but with encouragement from Mother, the milk started streaming out of the cow and into the bucket. "Look at that little Willard milk," Mother announced, loud enough for Dad to hear as I strained to squeeze out more milk. When the pail was half full, Dad said he would finish stripping the cow. I strutted from the barn to tell my younger sister Sylvia that I had milked a cow. After that I was expected to milk the same cow each morning and evening, and so I had advanced to another task. I really felt proud because now I was doing barn work.

We had about nine cows; my parents each milked two or three cows and we three older kids were expected to milk one apiece. Mother was a fast milker, quickly finishing her two cows and returning to the house to prepare breakfast. By the time Dad and we boys had completed the rest of the chores, Mother would have breakfast ready. By then we had been up for an hour or more and were hungry as wolves.

I still remember coming into the house, washing my hands, and running to the kitchen to see what was cooking. About once a week Mother had a foot-high stack of buckwheat cakes, which I loved, sitting in the warmer of the old range. Other mornings it might be johnnycakes, a form of pancakes made with cornmeal, flour, baking soda, and sour milk. With johnnycakes we ate oatmeal or some other hot cereal. You held a johnnycake covered with lots of apple butter in your left hand and ate oatmeal with your right, alternating bites. Some mornings we ate fried or scrambled eggs, lots of greasy fried potatoes, toast and perhaps bacon, if there was any left from the last butchering. In the fall season, our favorite breakfast was fried squash with tomato gravy. I still occasionally make myself a breakfast of this delicious meal.

We couldn't, however, sit down and immediately start eating. As Amish we waited until the whole family was seated at the table, then we bowed our heads in silent prayer. When Dad raised his head, it meant that the praying was done and we dove for the food. Sometimes I peeked; when Dad's head started to rise, I got a jump on the rest, spearing some buckwheats.

It didn't matter if you finished eating first, you sat at the table and waited until everyone was done. Dad was a slow eater; we kids often fidgeted, waiting for him to finish. His last act was to take a slice of bread and sl-o-o-o-wly wipe his plate clean, then announce, "Let's pray." As soon as the prayer was completed, we kids rushed from the table.

During the school year, one of us watched for the school bus, which we called a *hack*. From our rear living room window we could see the hack arrive at the Yoares's place, about three-quarters of a mile away. The bus had a number of stops and a few miles to go before it reached the end of our lane. When the bus watcher yelled, "Hack's comin'!" everyone grabbed his coat and lunch pail and went flying out the door. By half running and fast walking we would arrive at the end of our long lane a few minutes before the bus arrived about 7:30 A.M. We had been up two hours.

I did not start school until I was nearly seven, as the Amish didn't believe their kids should attend school beyond the eighth grade. Indiana law required all children to attend school until age sixteen; therefore the Amish often started their kids as late as the law would allow in order to keep them out of high school. They believed that eight years of school would provide their children with an adequate education needed to conduct a farming operation. Some Amish parents encouraged their children to flunk eighth grade and repeat it rather than advance to high school.

As Amish we dressed in plain clothes. In the Clay-Miami public school there were other Amish kids, as well as a few Mennonites, who also dressed plainly. This part of Indiana had consolidated its public schools about 1920, so we did not attend the small one-room schools our parents had. The Clay-Miami school was a big brick building that had rooms for all grades from one through twelve.

When I started school I knew very little English but had picked up enough from my older brother and sister to understand the teacher. We Amish were a minority in this school and were often teased by some of the other students because of the way we dressed. Since we were always aware we were different from other people, I have gained a little insight into how other minorities must feel.

I don't remember much about the two and a half years I spent at Clay-Miami school, but my second grade teacher left an indelible impression. In the spring after a long winter, when the migrating birds began to return to Indiana, she asked if anyone had seen a robin. When one student raised his hand, she wrote *robin* on the blackboard, with the student's name beside it. The next day it might be *bluebird, house wren, barn swallow,* or *Baltimore oriole*. It sparked a tremendous interest in me and, with a little help from my mother who also liked birds, it set the stage for my lifelong interest in nature, particularly birds.

My brother Joel was also interested. One day while leafing through a farm magazine, he noticed an ad for Arm & Hammer Baking Soda. The fine print of the ad said that if you sent it in to get information on their product, you would also receive a set of colored bird cards. Immediately we paged through every magazine in the house, clipped the Arm & Hammer ads and sent them off in the mail. Soon we had a stack of colored bird cards. Those sets were our only bird guide for many years.

In the evening when we returned from school, it was again time for chores. We first had to change from our school to work clothes. These were usually garments that Mother had patched many times. We were hungry, as our school lunch had been meager compared to the big noon meal served at home, so we sneaked cookies, crackers, and apples from the pantry to tide us over until supper. We boys headed to the barn, climbed into the mow, and pitched down hay and straw for the horses and cows. The cow parlor had to be mucked out. We forked manure out the small doors behind the cow stalls. Often quite a pile developed before Dad or we boys loaded it in the manure spreader and hauled it to the fields for fertilizer. After we removed the manure we placed fresh straw on the floor for the cows. Then we fed the young calves and placed feed in the troughs for the horses and cows.

During spring, summer, and fall one of us had to get the cows that were kept in the back pasture. Our collie dog Trixie was good at rounding up the cows on our command. Nipping at their heels, he soon had them lined out and headed for the barn. Sometimes Almeda would get the cows; she liked the change from housework. The girls were responsible for helping Mother get supper ready, gathering the eggs, and getting produce from the garden.

By 5:30 or so Joel and I would run the cows in and lock them in their stanchions. Each cow had her own stall. When we opened the door, they streamed in knowing their feed box would have a delicious meal; it contained ground corn and oats supplemented with other products to encourage milk production. The stanchions were two long vertical boards, each carved out in a half-circle in the center, forming a hole when the hinged boards were locked into place; the cow could move her neck up and down but couldn't pull her head back out. Sometimes one of the cows would get in the wrong stall, often in a deliberate attempt to eat the other cow's feed. This always caused a rumpus, and Joel and I would yell and crack the whip to get them in the right place. Once we had slammed the stanchions shut, they settled down. Then the whole family showed up to do the evening milking.

Each family member milked the same cows he or she had milked in the morning. Our cows all had names, so everyone knew if they were to milk Minnie, Star, Daisy, Royal, or Spot. Some were gentle; others had a tendency to kick. The small kids always milked the gentle cows and Dad got the kickers. When you heard him yell, "Ya stupid, rotten, *alte kuh*! I'll teach you!" and his milk stool hit the cow, you knew she had tried to kick him or had stepped into the milk pail.

The pail was held between your legs while you sat on a one-legged stool. If the cow was gentle the pail could sit flat on the floor. A good milk cow would fill a three-gallon bucket twice a day, while others had only a gallon to give. Some cows produced richer milk than others.

After we finished milking a cow, we poured the milk into five- or ten-gallon cans, which were then hauled to the milk house. Until I was twelve years old we sold cream on the market rather than whole milk, so all our milk was run through a milk separator, segregating the cream from the skim milk. This was one of the last chores we had to do before going to the house for supper. We put the skimmed milk into large crocks and allowed it to ferment. The sour milk on top was for the chickens, and the whey—the liquid under the sour milk—we fed to the hogs.

Supper was often a big meal, similar to *middagessa,* our noon meal, and sometimes consisted of lots of meat, gravy, potatoes, and other vegetables. In the winter when there wasn't as much hard physical labor, supper was soup with pickles, relishes, and beets.

One of my favorite suppers was bean soup. Mom dumped cooked navy beans into a pot of hot milk and crumbled bread. A large dipper sat in the soup and we all filled our bowls as many times as we desired. In the summer when it was hot, the soup was fruit: strawberries, raspberries, or mulberries, mixed with cold milk and thickened with crumbled bread. I still like it today, but my kids say, "Yuck!"

After the meal and prayer were over, the girls cleared the table and we kids took turns washing dishes. While we worked, Mother often sat in her rocker darning socks or mending clothes while supervising our getting the dishes done. Often she led us in singing hymns to make the boring chore go faster. When my younger sisters got older and began to do dishes, I usually got out of it. Joel and I considered it women's work.

It was usually about 7:30 by the time the last chore was done. Sometimes we got to read by the light of a kerosene lamp until 8:00 or 8:30 P.M., and then it was off to bed because morning came early. Chores were routine but had to be done, especially the milking; the cows had to be milked twice a day, seven days a week, 365 days a year.

3

HORSE POWER

"Giddyup, giddyup!" the driver commands. With a gentle slap of the lines, the team of horses responds as one. They lean into their collars, necks bowed, manes flying, muscles rippling. The traces strain and creak as the team moves the heavy load forward. The pair works together like scullers pulling their oars in perfect unison.

There were nearly 20 million draft horses in the U.S. around World War I; they provided nearly all the power for tilling the soil on American farms. These heavy breeds had helped clear the forests and plow up the prairies during America's westward expansion. The lighter breeds provided horseback transportation and pulled stagecoaches and buggies before the age of the automobile.

Large draft horses have given way to tractors, but in my early youth, horses were still the main source of power on our family farm. Nearly every Amish farm kid admired horses, loved to watch them work, and delighted in riding and driving them. I was no exception.

My earliest memory, at the age of three, was of a horse. For some unknown reason one of our large draft horses died in the back pasture one night. The next morning I climbed up on the wooden barn gate to get a better look at the dead animal. The day was a sad one for our family as we watched the *stink truck* come. The driver got out and tied a large rope to the horse's leg, then winched the animal aboard the truck. Calling the stink truck was never a pleasant chore. It didn't happen often, but when we lost a cow, horse, pig, or sheep, the truck came and hauled the animal away to be converted into fertilizer.

Nearly all my memories of horses, however, are happy ones. As soon as I could run, I followed my father in the fields while he was working a team of horses. At the end of the day when he unhitched the team from a plow, mower, or other implement, he would let me hold the horses' lines as we headed back to the barn. Occasionally, he would toss me up on the back of gentle old Bell and tell me to grab the hames and hang on as we proceeded home. I could see all the world from the top of that high horse and felt like a little king. I longed for the day when I could drive a team in the field by myself.

That day came when I was six years old. I was always eager to feed the horses and pet them; whenever I could, I went with Dad and sat beside him while he drove a team. He saw my keen interest in horses and encouraged me to take the lines, just as many modern farmers let their kids steer the tractor. Gradually I became proficient at driving the horses.

One day my father asked if I thought I could drive the team hitched to a cultipacker. Could I! "*Ya, ich konn,*" I confidently answered.

We had two gentle draft horses called Bell and Prince. Dad knew they could do the fieldwork almost by themselves. The cultipacker was a long narrow implement eight feet across, made of a double set of small steel wheels that were slightly grooved at intervals. Pulled over a plowed and harrowed field, it pulverized the clods of dirt.

My father hitched the team to the cultipacker and we drove out into the field. He sat on the seat while I stood between his legs on a wooden plank that covered the steel frame; I leaned back against him so I wouldn't fall off. He made several turns around the field and told me exactly how to follow the edge of the previous cultipacker line. "Ya sink ya can do it?" he asked.

"Ya! Ya!" I said.

I was nervous and my heart was thumping when he got off the implement and handed me the lines. "Aw right."

He stood nearby and anxiously watched my first move. The horses knew more about cultipacking than I did, and when I said "Giddyup!" in my small voice, they responded. Slowly they plodded around the field, the outside horse walking on the edge of the previously packed soil. It was a small field near the house and I'm sure Dad kept an eye on my efforts from a distance. As I drove the horses round and round the field, the turns gradually became shorter. Occasionally Bell failed to walk a straight line and I tried to correct her by pulling on the harness lines. In spite of my efforts, the straight border became a series of zigzag curves and I was having a hard time following the edges. Finally, in tears, I stopped the horses, walked back to the house and told my dad the problem. He went back to the field with me and showed me how to cut across the crooked lines until everything was straight again.

At noon my father came to the field and helped me unhitch the horses and drive them to the barn for rest and feed. We then went to the house for dinner. Mother was helping a neighbor with some canning and wasn't home that day. The only thing Dad could cook was eggs. Our dinner consisted of fried eggs, applesauce, and bread, the standard meal when Mother was gone. I was still a bit hungry, so I walked into the pantry and found half an apple pie left from Mom's weekend pie baking. Dad and I polished it off in a hurry.

After dinner I went back to the field with the horses, and toward mid-afternoon the rounds really started to get short. Bell and Prince sensed that we were nearly through and responded by walking faster and faster. When I finished, I drove the team to the gate entrance, and then I walked to the barn to tell Dad. "All done, already?" he asked, then praised my efforts. "Pretty soon ya gonna be able ta do all da field work for me!"

My buttons about popped off my shirt; I was so proud that I had driven a team in the field by myself. When Mother came home, I wasted no time in telling her I had cultipacked the field with Bell and Prince. "Say, you're quite a little man," she said.

That evening after supper I got a rope, hitched my sisters together into a make-believe horse team, and drove them around the living room. My sisters encouraged my expanded ego as they pranced and galloped around the room until it was bedtime.

It wasn't long before I graduated to other field projects with the horses. I was eager to try new things, and Dad always encouraged me to advance to another job. Soon I was driving teams of horses mowing hay, dragging a spike-toothed harrow, and doing other complicated field projects. Eventually Dad taught me to handle three or four horses hitched together while disking or plowing. By the time I was ten, I could do nearly everything with the horses my father did.

That is, everything but harness them.

Getting the harness on a team of horses required a lot of muscle and a bit of height. I was just too short in my britches to accomplish the job. Horses also had to be curried in the morning before they were harnessed. I learned to do this in spite of my height. I put a small wooden box along the side of a horse; standing on my tiptoes on top of the box, I could reach the horse's high shoulders and run the currycomb along its back. This smoothed its coat and got the dirt and grime out of its hair, preventing sores from developing under the collar and harness. Some of the gentle ones even lowered their heads so I could currycomb their necks.

After currying a horse, Dad would put a soft pad and leather collar over its neck and slide it against the horse's shoulder. This was where all the horsepower was concentrated when it pulled the load. He would then load the harness onto his shoulder, walk alongside of the horse, and toss it onto the horse's back. The steel hames fit into a groove on the leather collar and were cinched tight by fastening a buckle on the bottom. Then the harness was stretched over the horse's back with the end going under the tail and the straps fastened under the belly until the harness was secure. The last step was to put on the bridle. Sometimes the horse didn't like to have the steel bit slipped into its mouth, and Dad had to force the clenched teeth open. But the bit was essential for controlling the horse with the lines when driving. The harnessing process took about ten minutes.

In addition to the large powerful draft horses, each Amish family kept one or two of the lighter horse breeds to pull the buggy. Most families took pride in having a rather spirited fast trotter. My folks had two buggy horses. We often used one or both of them as a dual-purpose horse. On Sundays we hitched them to the buggy to take us to church; during the week we used them with the draft horses to help do the fieldwork.

When I was seven or eight, I heard about the cowboys of the west who practically lived on horses, herding and chasing cattle over the wide-open ranges. Becoming a cowboy seemed like the ultimate career to me. One day I vaguely mentioned my goal to my mother. She quickly replied, "Amish don't do those 'English' things. Cowboying is only for the *hoche*," which was the way she referred to anyone not Amish.

That put a damper on my planned cattle-herding career, but I continued to admire the cowboys on their horses. One day I noticed a cowboy suit for small boys advertised in the Sears Roebuck Catalog. I dreamed of owning such a suit and fantasized myself riding atop a galloping horse in the fancy outfit. But I knew wearing such clothing was taboo for us. I also noticed the suit cost $1.00, a prohibitive price, since I had only twenty-five pennies in my piggy bank. My cowboy life would have to be delayed.

I also wanted a Shetland pony, as did most farm kids. My folks thought ponies were fine, but this was during the Depression and we could not afford one. "Maybe some day," my dad told me. For the time being, I would have to be content with occasionally riding old Bell and driving horses in the field.

Horses were a practical source of power on the farm. For fuel you fed them corn, oats, and hay and grazed them in the field. Then you put their manure back on the fields for fertilizer to produce better crop yields. It was a perfect cycle. There was little cash outlay for their upkeep.

There were other advantages to using horses. In contrast to a noisy tractor that constantly pummeled your ears, the only sounds you heard while driving a team of horses were the occasional creak of the harness or the slight squeak of an implement wheel that might need some grease. You could hear the low, barely audible rumble as the plow turned over the soil. When you stopped at the end of the field to rest the horses, you listened to the birds singing in a nearby tree or to the geese honking overhead in the spring of the year. Cows lowed in the distance, and in the stillness of an Indiana summer day you could sometimes hear the neighbors talking. You became more attuned to nature by working with horses. When I rested the animals I often watched the fleecy clouds roll by and dreamed of soaring in the sky. I learned to tell time by the sun. I didn't need a watch; when the sun was directly overhead, I knew it was noon and time for dinner. I rarely missed the time by more than fifteen minutes.

Horses, efficient and quiet, provided a personal relationship impossible with a tractor. It took more time to farm with horses, but in many ways it was more rewarding, as I was to find out later.

4

THE NEIGHBORHOOD

Good neighbors were essential to every successful farmer; they were like an extended family. If you got sick, they were there to help. During the busy periods, neighbors helped each other with manpower, horsepower, and equipment. When I was young, very few farms were completely self-sufficient. Most farmers could not afford all the implements needed to run their business; instead they borrowed or shared equipment with neighbors. One farmer might borrow a hayrake, hay loader, or extra wagon from you. In exchange, you borrowed a grain binder or extra plow as you needed it. During the busy haying season, neighbors worked together putting up hay on one farm for a few days, then doing the same on another farm the following week. It all worked out to the benefit of everyone and made for a lot of close social ties between families.

Our closest neighbors were Levi and Mary Ann Sommers, who lived near the end of our long lane. We shared a boundary line fence with the Sommers and their four children: Floyd, Ralph, Clara, and Lydia. They were not Amish, but we did not consider them 'English.' They spoke the Pennsylvania Dutch dialect just like we did and belonged to the Conservative Church, which was less conservative than the Amish. They dressed plainly; Levi had a beard and a big black hat like my dad's, but their more liberal religion allowed them to use electricity and to own a car and a telephone, taboo in our home. Mary Ann was a distant cousin to my mother. Mom often said, "They are just like us Amish."

Now, maybe my parents didn't covet the Sommers' telephone, but they sure used it a lot. That was probably our main reason for visiting them. It was a hand-crank model with which you rang so many longs or shorts to get a neighbor or the operator. The reception was not the best, so the caller often shouted into the phone. It was hard to keep your phone conversations private, for even if folks were in another room, they could still hear one end of the conversation. Using the Sommers' telephone was also a good excuse to chat, so our trips there were rarely short.

Mary Ann was quite a talker and seemed to live on the pessimistic side of life. A typical exchange between her and Mother might go like this: "Well, hello, Mary Ann, how are you today?" Mom would say.

"Oh, I don't know, Katy, *Ich glaub ich kann nicht snaffa* (I believe I'm just about ready to quit breathing.)"

"Now, Mary Ann, you sure look healthy to me."

"No, I think I'm gonna just lie down on the sofa one of these days and die."

My mother would change the subject, and Mary Ann would soon forget about dying and start relating some choice piece of gossip with fiery delight. I know my mother enjoyed her, because as we walked home she would chuckle about Mary Ann's doleful outlook on life and tell us children that Mrs. Sommers was as healthy as any energetic teenager.

Levi was a large, strong man with a slight paunch and many talents. Because he was a good sausage maker and knew how to cure and smoke good hams, he always helped us with hog butchering. Levi not only operated his small farm with his two sons, he was also a carpenter and a preacher. He plied his carpenter trade wherever his skills were needed, building barns and farmhouses throughout the community. As was typical of Amish, Conservative, and Mennonite churches, being a preacher was an honorary thing and a duty; one did not get paid for being a minister and doing the extra work that went with this obligation.

I was always impressed with son Ralph's knowledge of nature. He was about five years older than I. In his room he had a sample from nearly every hardwood tree that grew in the woods, neatly cut and labeled. He also knew a lot about birds and small animals. Occasionally I went to the woods with him and watched as he hunted fox squirrels.

We had an Amish neighbor just south of us. She was a widow named Ale Kate Miller. I don't know how long she had been a widow or what happened to her husband, but she had two boys named Dan and Jekkie (Jakey). She was fairly self-sufficient and, in spite of not having a husband, did a successful job of running her farm with her two teenage sons. They had a hayrake, which my dad borrowed during the haying season. It was one of those side-delivery rakes that rolled the loosely cut hay into long rows. The wagon and hay loader could then straddle the rows, and the loader could push hay onto the wagon. It was faster and easier than hand pitching the hay up on a high wagon to haul to the barn.

Like Mary Ann, Ale Kate was also quite a talker. Her house sat near the road and, if she was in her garden or yard, my mom always stopped the horse and buggy to chat awhile.

We also shared a boundary fence line with our back neighbor, Earl Agnes. He had a number of children, but I did not know them well, as they were older than I. Besides being in our threshing ring during grain harvesting season, our main association with Earl was his dairy bull. We had about eight or nine dairy cows at that time and no bull; whenever one of our milkers came in heat and needed to be bred, my dad took the cow to the Earl Agnes farm to have a little romance with their bull. Dad never told us kids why he was taking the cow to the neighbors. He always said, "I'm gonna take Minnie (or Brindle or Spot) for a valk. You kids stay home."

If we asked why he was taking the cow for a walk, he was very evasive. My parents never talked to us about the birds and the bees, and the word sex was taboo, yet we kids were exposed to all kinds of natural reproduction. Roosters were always jumping the hens, buck sheep bred ewes, and old boars climbed aboard the sows and stayed there awhile. All kinds of breeding antics went on all around us, but our parents never talked about the subject. If we were caught watching a boar on top of a sow, my parents would say, "Now, you don't need to watch dat! Now git away from dere."

We knew a lot, however, at an early age. One of our Amish cousins, Neely Miller, was well informed by his two older brothers and he in turn kept my brother Joel and me apprised of the birds and the bees. He often told us long, lurid tales about human sex as well as the details of animal reproduction. So we knew plenty, though we pretended ignorance of the subject around our folks. They apparently thought we would learn soon enough, and we did.

Another Amish family, the Planks, lived just north of Levi Sommers. Mr. Plank repaired watches as a sideline to farming. His wife had a home remedy for making tea from sheep droppings. She made her kids drink the putrid brew when they were sick. Mother thought this was really disgusting and told her so. We didn't associate with them too much; I think Mother was afraid Mrs. Plank might try to serve the tea on a social visit.

My mother had her own remedies she used in treating us kids when we became sick. She gathered wild pennyroyal from our woods and dried the leaves. The tea was used for medicinal purposes as well as a social drink for adults. Pennyroyal, a wild mint, has a pleasing aroma when steeped in hot water. If we got a cold or flu, Mom prepared the hot tea for us to drink. She also covered a steaming cup of tea with a heavy slitted paper, then had us place our nose next to the slit and deeply inhale the hot steam up our nostrils. It was supposed to clear our sinuses, and it did. I still use this remedy today. For a bad chest cold or a sore throat, Mother used a medicinal sticky plaster spread on a heavy cloth, which she heated, then placed on our chest and throat. She wrapped us in a heavy scarf and sent us to bed. She also had a recipe for a blood poison salve that she applied to every cut or skin puncture we got while running around barefoot all summer. If we had loose bowels, she made us take wild dried camellia buds. Our mother also forced cod-liver oil down our throats. It was a popular cure for nearly everything. Just the thought of that awful-tasting stuff usually resulted in us kids getting well in a hurry.

To the northeast near McGrawsville lived Treat Morton, another 'English' neighbor. He was the only person I knew as a child who had been to a foreign country. He was a soldier during World War I, serving in France. After the war he stayed with a German family as part of the occupation forces for one year and learned a little German. He often tried his High German on my folks, which, according to my mom, almost made him *one of us*. Treat had a large farm and a huge woods filled with maple trees. During the spring he gathered maple sap and boiled it down into syrup. I went with my dad several times to visit Treat in his sugaring shed. It was set deep in the middle of the biggest woods I had ever seen. There were songbirds flitting about the trees, while fox and pine squirrels chased each other through the big hickory and walnut trees. It was about as wild a place as I had ever experienced, and I thought it would be a great place to live when I grew up. Treat's maple trees were the source of the maple syrup we poured over our buckwheats for breakfast.

One summer Treat Morton's daughter Martha had a family of pet skunks living under her porch. She played with them like kittens. I admired the little skunks, but my mother warned me, "Now, Willard, don't go near those skunks! They'll squirt in your eyes and blind you, and if they miss your eyes and hit you elsewhere, you'll stink for weeks. You'll hafta live in the barn with the pigs if you mess with those skunks."

I stayed away.

Every rural neighborhood had a small town where the nearby farmers did their basic trading. Our small town of McGrawsville was about a mile from home and just past Treat Morton's place. It had a large grain elevator and a small general store owned by Mr. Overman. McGrawsville had a few homes, one church, and a railroad that ran through the middle of town. My parents did most of their small trading in this little railroad town. Dad sold his grain to the elevator and my parents bought a few essentials at the store. We kids often rode on the wagon with Dad when he hauled grain to the elevator. One day Mr. Overman told us to walk over to the store, then winked at my dad. The store manager was giving away free ice cream cones. We shyly entered the store. The manager looked at us kids and asked, "Would you kids like a cone?" We nodded our heads, too bashful to try our English.

I had never eaten a store-bought ice cream cone and was absolutely amazed as we ate the ice cream and the container it came in. When I got home, I told my mother, "Guess what! I had an ice cream cone and ate the box, too!"

We occasionally made ice cream at home with our hand-crank freezer. My dad would buy a block of ice for a few cents when he was in McGrawsville on a hot summer day, then we would make a freezer full and enjoy the cool taste.

It took a while to make ice cream. Dad placed the block of ice in a gunnysack; then we boys crushed it into small pieces by pounding it with a sledge. In the meantime, Mother mixed together milk, cream, eggs, sugar, a touch of salt, and some cheese rennet, and poured the ingredients into the tall, round steel can that sat inside the ice cream maker. The can was fastened into place, then the space between the can and the outer part of the round freezer was filled with crushed ice, layered with rock salt. The salt caused the ice to partially melt and lower the temperature, which cooled the ice cream contents in the can. We kids took turns cranking the ice cream maker. Soon one of us would yell, "It's gittin' hard."

This brought Mother out on the run to check and see if the ice cream was finished. She could tell by turning the crank. "Now you jist keep crankin' a little longer," was the usual reply.

Eventually it hardened and Mother would say, "Now, let it sit awhile, it'll harden more."

We hungry kids couldn't wait long and clamored for Mother to open it up. When she took off the lid and pulled out the paddles, we all gathered around, cleaning them off with our fingers and licking the delicious soft ice cream. Then Mother dipped out huge bowls for each of us. It was our favorite dessert.

More often we made it when the stock tank froze over during the cold winter, providing us with free ice. We chopped out the ice, made the dessert, then sat around the heating stove to keep our teeth from chattering as we ate the cold ice cream. One year, we had a storm in June that dropped hailstones as big as hen eggs. As soon as the storm was over, we raked up the hail, then chased in a few cows for fresh milk and made a freezer full of ice cream. We never let a resource go to waste.

Ice cream making was often a social event with our neighbors. Each family brought their hand-crank freezer, which added up to several gallons. The adults sat around and visited while we kids hand-cranked the freezer. The ice cream social filled our stomachs and our social needs, breaking the monotony of everyday farm life.

Besides getting the few essentials in McGrawsville, my parents made a trip to the city of Peru about twice a year with the horse and buggy. It was in this city that they paid their county taxes. We kids rarely got to go on this trip as Mom and Dad had a long list of things they had to do. Besides paying taxes, they bought staples such as flour, sugar, salt, and baking powder. Dad usually had a number of implement or horse harness parts to buy. While there, Mom also bought cloth and other supplies to make clothes for the family. They always returned late in the evening. We were glad to see them come, because we usually got a few candy treats.

One day they did take all of us kids to Peru to see the circus animals. In those days the winter quarters of the Beck and Wallace Circus were in Peru. They kept all their unique animals on the grounds and nearby farms. We got to see lions, tigers, giraffes, elephants, and other kinds of exotic animals. While we were watching the lions, one of the big males let out a loud roar. It scared me and I bolted toward the gate, but Mom caught me. I told her I didn't want to go near that lion again. We talked about the experience for weeks afterward.

I always wanted to see a circus when it was performing in town, but Mom said, "Amish don't go ta those kinda things. They're for the 'English.'"

We had other neighbors, both Amish and 'English,' who lived farther down the road, but it was with our close neighbors that we did most of our socializing and working together. Since you had to either walk or go by horse and buggy, traveling very far took too much time out of your busy farm day.

5

GOING TO PREACHING

The nucleus of Amish society is the church or church district. The district usually consists of twenty-five to forty families. The Amish do not have their service in a church building but meet in each other's homes. If an Amish neighborhood becomes too large, the church district is split so everyone can fit into a house or barn during the preaching service. The service is held every other Sunday, and everyone attends. We children were never given a choice of attending or staying home.

Preparations for the Sunday service always started on Saturday evening when everyone took the weekly bath to be clean for church. Since we did not have indoor plumbing, we heated the hand-pumped water on the kitchen range, then poured it into a big galvanized tub in the pump house. This served as the bathhouse. The pump house was unheated and a co-o-o-ld place during the winter months. You got in and out of the tub in a hurry! The water didn't get changed after every bath, so we children often argued over who would get to go first. None of us relished bathing in someone else's dirty water.

On Sunday morning we did our chores and had breakfast, then everyone got into his Sunday clothes. We boys wore our dark pants with big front flaps, light-colored shirts, dark coats, and big black hats, while Mom and the girls dressed in their best plain-colored dresses, shawls, and dark bonnets.

Dad always hitched our two fast trotters to the family buggy and tied them to the horse rail in front of the house. As soon as we were dressed, the family climbed into the buggy. Dad, Mom, and the baby sat in the front seat, and the rest of us occupied the rear. By 8:00 or 8:30 A.M. we were on our way to the preaching service.

One Sunday morning as everyone scrambled aboard, Dad grabbed the reins, slapped the horses on the rump, and we were off. Ben and Minor always stepped out snappily when hitched to a buggy. They seemed to prefer trotting down the road to pulling some slow implement in the field the way they had to do during the rest of the week. The steady *clip-clop, clip-clop* of their shod feet hitting the solid gravel road resounded throughout the quiet neighborhood.

As we arrived at the first crossroad, the Beachy and Yoder buggies approached from the right and, in the distance ahead, five or six more buggies were plodding toward preaching service. Just as we passed the crossroad, the Beachy family buggy gained some speed and swung in closely behind us. Normally an Amishman wouldn't think of passing another buggy, especially on Sunday. It was considered showing off. But for some reason the Beachy horses started moving along our left side until their team were even with our front buggy wheels. I saw Mose Beachy grin at my dad as they were gaining on our buggy. Dad must have had a competitive streak in him this Sunday morning, and he lightly slapped the lines on the horses' rumps. Our buggy surged ahead. Mose Beachy reciprocated and now suddenly we had four horses clippity-clopping down the road at a very fast pace. As the Beachy buggy gained, Dad again slapped the lines. We now had a real race going! We kids stuck our heads out the side of the buggy and waved at the Beachy kids. Everyone was grinning and pumping their arms. "Now, Mart, *du bist ferrooked* (You're acting crazy)," Mom said, but since she was chuckling, we all knew she had caught the racing spirit.

The horses also recognized the contest and the two teams raced neck and neck down the road. The horses' legs were flying and the fast clippity-clop now sounded like the rapid beat of a drummer's roll. Minor was a pacer, and his legs were swinging back and forth like the whirring spokes on a wheel. We were gaining on the other slow buggies ahead and something had to give soon. Each team was trotting at its utmost speed; sometimes one surged ahead for a few feet, then the other picked up the pace. But slowly the Beachy buggy started creeping past ours, to the disappointment of us kids. Mom was still scolding Dad, "Now Mart…now Mart…after all, this is Sunday!"

But Dad hated to lose and again gave a snappy slap on the horses' rumps. Well, this time old Ben responded by breaking into a full gallop. Boy, oh boy, were we flying! Joel and I were yelling, "Go, Dad, go!" and jumping up and down in the rear of the buggy.

But galloping was not exactly a pious Amish way to go to church, and

Dad was forced to rein in our horses so Ben would get back to a trotting mode. That gave the Beachy team a chance to pull ahead of us. The race was suddenly over. We boys groaned with disappointment and sat back down. The drivers reined in their teams and we both fell in behind the buggies ahead and proceeded to the preaching at normal horse speed.

As we approached the home where the preaching service was to be held, there was a line of a dozen buggies moving along the long lane toward the house. Another twelve or fifteen were already pulled up near the barn. Horses were slowed to a walk, then stopped near the house, where the women and girls got out. The men drove the buggies to the barn. Several young Amish boys unhitched the horses, led them into the barn, tied them in a stall, and gave them some hay. When that was done, all the men and boys gathered in groups, shook hands, and visited. They were uniformly dressed in their dark suits, light shirts, and big broad-brimmed black hats. I saw Dad edge up to Mose Beachy, nudge his elbow in Mose's side, and whisper, "You got fast horses."

Mose and my dad grinned at each other. It was Dad's way of saying, "You won this time."

One of the preachers announced it was time to head to the house. The bishop, deacons, and preachers went first, followed by old men; then middle-aged married men came with their small boys in tow, and the teenage boys went last. Just before entering the house all the men hung their big black hats on racks on the side of the house that had been installed for that purpose. Soon the wall of the white house was lined with circular black hats. My brother Joel and I hung our small hats beneath Dad's.

On the other side of the house, the women were also filing in by age group. The women with small babies went in last so they could sit in the back in case the youngsters started crying and they had to leave the room. The women placed their big dark bonnets and heavy shawls in the washhouse as they entered.

Most Amish houses are designed with the preaching service in mind. Large removable partitions between rooms allow more space. Men and women sit in different rooms or on different sides of the house, while the preachers sit near the middle partition. The house is filled with long, hard wooden benches.

Members take turns hosting the preaching service. On Friday neighboring women get together to bake pies and prepare the food that will be served after the service. The man of the house goes for the church benches, which are stored at the house that held the previous preaching service. Early Sunday morning the benches are placed in the house or barn. During the summer, preaching is often held in the barn, especially when the house is small. I can remember chickens clucking, roosters crowing, and cows mooing while church was underway. This may not have distracted the adults, but it broke the church service routine for me as I turned my head to get a glimpse of the livestock.

Preaching service starts about 9 A.M. and is conducted the same way each time. Everyone sits in silence for a few minutes. Then one of the older men announces a hymn and starts to sing what seems like a solo for the first long drawn-out syllable, after which the rest join in. The songs, from a hymnal first printed in Europe around 1600, are sung slowly in regular German, not Pennsylvania Dutch. To an outsider it can sound more like a wail or chanting as the words are drawn out, often syllable by syllable. Everyone sings in unison, and sometimes it takes twenty minutes to sing one hymn.

When the singing begins, the preachers file upstairs or to another room to conduct church business and decide who will preach the main sermon. In the meantime singing continues with long silences between songs. The *vorsinger* (first song leader) nods or nudges another man to pass on the responsibility of leading the next hymn. As a small child I didn't know the slow complicated hymns, so I rarely participated in the singing.

When the preachers are through with their business meeting, they file downstairs and the singing soon stops. One of the preachers delivers the first sermon, which rarely lasts more than thirty minutes. It is followed by a silent prayer with everyone kneeling. At the end of the prayer, the group stands while the deacon reads portions of the Bible. The main sermon follows and usually lasts an hour and a half; it is conducted in a singsong manner, the preacher's voice rising and falling dramatically.

All the services are conducted in High German and small kids who understand only Pennsylvania Dutch and perhaps English are not able to understand the preachers. Later, young children receive instruction in German so that they too can comprehend.

By the beginning of the main sermon we small children were tired and fidgety. The backless benches were hard and because I was so short, my feet couldn't touch the floor unless I let myself slide down. Every time I did, Dad would pull me back on the bench and tell me, "*Sitz.*"

About this time in the service the Amish ladies would pass cookie plates to all the families with small kids to ease our hunger and break the monotony. I remember one day when Joel and I both took two cookies. Bored with the sermon, which I couldn't understand, and sore from sitting on the hard bench, I looked for entertainment. A few flies buzzed around my cookies, so I set a trap for them. I held a small piece of cookie between my thumb and forefinger. When a fly landed, I pinched my fingers shut, trapping the fly's legs. The fly made a buzzing sound as it fanned its wings in an attempt to get loose. I held it awhile, then released the fly and set the trap for another. By now there were lots of flies around. In a few minutes I had captured and released a half dozen. Soon I was no longer aware of the boring sermon or the hard benches. My brother Joel had also caught a few flies, and we raced to see who could catch the most.

Then the game took a dire turn for the flies. I was bored with catching and releasing them, so I plucked the wings off the next prisoner and dropped it to the floor. Soon I had six or seven wingless flies scurrying around by my feet. Finally my dad saw what was going on and gave me a hard nudge in the ribs. Now I had to sit and listen to the droning sound of the sermon, wondering if it would ever be over.

Finally the preaching was done and several members gave some approving statements on what had been said. There were a few closing remarks by the preacher and then another kneeling prayer. This gave me a chance to rest my weary bottom and stretch my legs. Next came the benediction and announcements. A final hymn was sung and the congregation was dismissed.

Boy, oh, boy! I could finally stand up and move around. It was one o'clock, and I was hungry! Some of the benches were replaced with tables, and the women filled them with pies, pickles, beets, relishes, bread, jams, apple butter, and coffee. The freshly ground coffee smelled good. Dad let us boys get a cup of the hot brew so we could dip our apple butter bread into it. I ate several slices before finishing with a big piece of *snitz* pie made from dried apples. After everyone was finished eating at our setting, another prayer was said and we left the table so the next group could eat.

Dad then let us boys meet some of our Amish buddies while he talked about crops and religion with the older men. Five or six of us seven- and eight-year-olds played in one of the buggies, telling each other what we had done the past week and making believe we were racing the buggy down the road.

Playing and eating were the parts of church I liked the best, and that time went fast. About 3:00 P.M. Dad went to the barn, hitched up Ben and Minor, then got us boys. Reluctantly we climbed into the buggy, got Mom and our sisters, and soon Ben and Minor were clip-clopping home.

This ritual was followed every other Sunday by all Amish families. On the Sunday when there was no preaching service, we still got dressed in our Sunday clothes and sat in the living room and listened to our parents read the Bible. In the summertime on the no-church Sunday we had Sunday school. It was a real school for us small kids as we were taught the German ABCs and how to read in the German language. By the time you were a teenager you could understand the High German preaching service or at least most of it. All Amish eventually become tri-lingual, speaking Pennsylvania Dutch at home, English with their 'English' neighbors, and listening to the High German preaching and reading the German Bible.

Some weeks when we did not have Sunday school, our family often visited neighbors or some of our cousins. Other times we stayed home and we kids played while our parents rested, preparing themselves for the new week to come. Sundays were a welcome change from the daily routine of farm life.

6

LATTWEICH TIME

The orchard in our McGrawsville farm had many apple trees and a lot of the fruit went into our stomachs. We kept a fresh supply in the root cellar that lasted most of the winter. Mother dried bushels of apples, canned many quarts, and filled dozens of jars with applesauce. Our favorite use of apples, however, was in the form of *lattweich* (apple butter). We had it on the table for every meal, just like butter. It took forty gallons each year to supply our family's need for this delicious spread. We seldom consumed a piece of bread that wasn't coated with a thick layer of lattweich, and sometimes we made apple butter sandwiches.

Making apple butter in the fall, when frost was on the ground and the maple trees had turned to gold and crimson, was an annual ritual. The key to this event was a big, round copper kettle, tapered at the bottom, with a huge handle, capable of holding thirty gallons or more. The kettle originally belonged to Mom's Uncle Dan. She got it from his estate sale soon after my parents were married. When Mom and Dad first purchased the copper kettle, they had a steel stand made, which consisted of a wide iron ring supported by three legs, in which the round-bottomed kettle sat. The stand kept the kettle several feet off the ground, leaving enough space to build a fire under it to heat the contents. The wide iron ring kept the flames from shooting up the sides of the kettle.

A wooden device fitted over the top of the kettle rim and held a shaft attached to huge paddles. These wooden paddles were formed to scrape along the bottom of the contoured kettle and keep the contents from burning. The paddle shaft was connected through a series of gears to a twelve-foot handle and crank. The long handle was necessary to keep the person turning the crank away from the hot coals.

Making lattweich was a big undertaking and nearly always involved a working social with the neighbors. Before the event, we picked five or six bushels of fresh apples from our orchard for peeling and slicing. We also gathered more apples of lesser quality (usually those that had fallen to the ground) for making cider.

We borrowed a cider press from our neighbor. The apples were cranked through a rough crusher, then placed between huge wooden plates layered with thick hemp cloth. The turning of a large crank attached to gears forced the wooden plates together squeezing the juice through the hemp cloth into a large tub below. We removed the remaining pulp and fed it to chickens and hogs. Some of the apple juice or partially fermented cider was added to the sliced apples in making apple butter; the rest we drank as fresh juice or allowed it to age for a few days to become tasty apple cider.

The night before making apple butter, we invited neighbors in for a *schnitzin'*, where everyone helped peel, core, and slice the apples. Before they arrived, we placed our large dining room table in the middle of the kitchen and spread chairs around it for the workers. Mother clamped an apple peeler on each end of the table. This device was a simple but ingenious tool invented in the 1800s. It had three prongs that held an apple firmly. As you cranked the handle, spinning the apple, a curved metal blade slid along the fruit, removing the peeling. Each apple was peeled in a few seconds, then tossed into a large pan. You reached into the basket, grabbed another, placed it on the peeler, turned the crank, and repeated the process. The rest of the group cored and sliced the skinned fruit.

One or two peelers and six to ten schnitzers sat around the table working rapidly, while laughing, joking, and gossiping. "Didja hear Jake kicked his ornery cow while he had on his knee boots and broke his toe?"

"No! Did he go see Dr. Kratzer?"

"No, he jist put a splint on it, but he hadda call the vet to fix the cow." Ha, ha, ha, ha…laughter erupted from around the table.

From Mary Ann…"Floyd has a new sweetheart."

"Oh," Mom wanted to know, "Is she Amish or Conservative?"

"No, she's an 'English' girl that he met at school, and a goot farm girl."

"Oh, I don't know about those *hoche* (worldly) girls," Mom said.

Mary Ann quickly changed the subject to Ale Kate's Duroc sow that had given birth to a litter of fifteen pigs.

When the last apples were peeled and sliced, Mom set out a half-dozen schnitz pies, a traditional dessert made from dried apples. They soon disappeared as the stories continued. By then we kids were running around outside, whooping and hollering, playing hide and seek, tag, leap frog, or just racing around the yard. About 8:30 or 9:00 P.M., the neighbors left and our parents ordered us to bed because tomorrow would be another busy day.

In the morning we set the copper kettle into its steel stand and poured the sliced apples into the kettle, along with some apple juice or cider, a little sugar, cinnamon, cloves, and allspice. Then we built a fire under the kettle with oak or hickory wood that turned into hot coals. When that was accomplished we kids took turns cranking the paddles. At first we fought to do the cranking, but a few hours later it became boring and we dreaded the work. The paddles had to be turned constantly, without pause, all day long. If they stopped for more than a few seconds, the sauce would start to burn on the bottom of the kettle. Hour after hour we cranked with Mother checking frequently to make sure we didn't goof off.

Gradually the ingredients got cooked, turning into a sloppy sauce. In late afternoon as the sauce started to thicken, Mom would check it periodically. She ladled out a few spoonfuls onto a platter in separate portions. If liquid seeped out, the sauce had to be cooked a little longer. When the portions remained separated, the fire was put out and the cranking ceased. The apple butter was ladled into gallon crocks and allowed to cool. Mother poured hot paraffin into the top of the jars to seal them. We then stored the containers in the cool root cellar. Each finished batch contained about twenty gallons of apple butter, half the family's need of forty gallons of lattweich eaten each year; the process was repeated twice a year.

When my parents retired from farming many years later, one of my first cousins bought the copper kettle. Eventually my brother Joel's oldest daughter Rachael and her husband Bob inherited it. They still use it for making the traditional lattweich and it has now been in the family for nearly a hundred years. Recently, while I was visiting my relatives in Indiana, I saw it hanging in Bob and Rachael's garage. On the wall above the kettle was pinned their recipe for making lattweich:

    4 bushels Macintosh apples
    2 cups sugar
    6 TSP cinnamon
    4 TSP allspice
    4 TSP cloves
    4 gallons of cider
    20 quarts old apple sauce

7

FOOD APLENTY

Most modern families are unaware of how much food they consume in the course of a year because they buy their groceries at the store on a daily or weekly basis. We, however, were well aware of how much it took to supply our family's annual needs. In the late fall after everything had been harvested, canned, butchered, and stored, the cellar was lined with hundreds of cans of vegetables, fruits, meats, and crocks of sauerkraut. Root cellar bins were bulging with potatoes, apples, onions, and other vegetables. It was an enormous amount of produce, and it would be our grocery store until the next summer when fresh vegetables again became available.

Fresh eggs, meat, and milk were products of our livestock, and from the milk Mother made butter and various cheeses. Our only purchases were sugar, salt, baking soda, baking powder, spices, and sometimes flour. We often took wheat from the farm to a local mill and had it ground into flour. Dad also ran wheat through a fine screen in his hammer mill in the barn. We cooked and ate the finely ground grain as graham for breakfast, and Mother made a form of grape-nut cereal from the same source. Shelled corn run through the mill became cornmeal that Mom used for making cornmeal mush and cornbread, staples in our diet.

A large garden produced all the vegetables and it received special care. We spread chicken manure, rich in nitrogen and other nutrients, onto the garden each spring and plowed it under to enrich the soil.

In addition to the garden, we had a truck-patch. This was a plot set aside in a nearby field for the purpose of growing the vegetables that took a lot of space, such as sweet corn, potatoes, and pumpkins. We rotated the plot to different locations each year.

As soon as the garden vegetables were ready in the summer, Mom and my sisters started canning. The variety of vegetables and fruits ripened at different times, so this was an ongoing process. First there were the early peas, strawberries, asparagus, and cauliflower; then as the summer progressed, various fruits, corn, and tomatoes ripened. Nearly two hundred quarts of canned tomatoes lined the shelves by fall. Tomato gravy with fried squash was a favorite meal, but we also used tomatoes in soups and mixed them with other vegetable dishes. Fried green tomatoes sprinkled with an ample amount of sugar was considered a delicacy. Tomatoes were definitely a major staple for our family, as were potatoes.

By late fall hundreds of jars of peaches, pears, plums, apples, squash, corn, and beans filled the shelves in the cellar. Mom and my sisters worked at canning on a daily and weekly basis. This was in addition to fixing meals, gardening, milking, washing, mending clothes, and cleaning house. They never had an idle moment. Occasionally Mother got together with other neighbor ladies to can. This satisfied a social need among isolated farm ladies and broke the monotony of the long farm workdays.

In addition Mother dried fruits and vegetables. She had a large flat galvanized container that covered the top of the big kitchen range. The inside of the shallow dryer was filled with water that simmered on the stove and dried the various fruits and vegetables that she placed on top of the container. She then put the dried contents in cloth sacks and hung them from the rafters in the basement.

The digging and storing of potatoes was a family affair that took place in the late fall when the frost was on the pumpkins. Dad had a digger pulled by two horses. It unearthed the potatoes and scattered them on top of the ground; then we kids picked and sorted them. Any bruised spuds were kept for immediate consumption or fed to the hogs. The potatoes were loaded onto a wagon, hauled to the root cellar, and stored in a bin. They would last until the following summer. Mashed potatoes and gravy was a major dinner and supper item. Thinly sliced fried potatoes topped with tomato gravy was a breakfast favorite. Baked potatoes, potato salad, potato soup, and even raw potatoes were other ways we utilized this abundant food source. In those days we had never heard of French fries or potato chips.

We also gathered hickory nuts and walnuts from our woods. The walnuts we put through a hand-cranked corn sheller to remove the heavy rind covering. In our school, you could always tell which boys had been harvesting walnuts by the dark stain on their hands that lasted for days. We gathered wild blackberries from the woods as well as pennyroyal tea. The leaves from this mint plant, dried and stored, supplied us with a delicious hot drink.

During the summer our only source of fresh meat was chickens. Mom usually butchered two for the table at least once a week. When I heard chickens squawking loudly, I knew we would have a fresh chicken dinner. Mom was not squeamish about killing chickens. In the back yard sat a block of wood with two protruding nails spaced an inch apart. Mom placed the chicken's neck between the nails, stretched out the doomed fowl, and whacked off its head with an ax. As soon as the decapitated chicken lay still, she dipped it in a bucket of hot water for a few seconds to facilitate removing the feathers. This process might sound cruel, but chickens were raised for eating so we never had any doubts or emotions about killing them. It was just part of life on the farm.

In the winter we butchered one large cow, one or two lambs, and several hogs. These provided us with fresh meat for a few weeks, but most of the meat was cured or canned since we didn't have the means to freeze it. The beef and lambs were processed easily by the family. Many farmers considered sheep low-class livestock and felt that mutton was inferior to beef or pork. Dad said it was because they didn't butcher them right. According to my father, if the wool touched the flesh during butchering, it tainted the meat. I ran from the barn whenever I saw Dad getting ready to slaughter a lamb; they seemed so innocent. I enjoyed eating the fresh meat, however.

Hogs were another matter. We never formed close relationships with pigs, and I wasn't troubled when Dad dispatched one for eating. Hog butchering required the help of neighbors, and it became a work social, just like making lattweich. Parents and kids all had tasks to perform at this event. Dad and Levi Sommers directed the operation.

Hog butchering was an all day affair. Early in the morning we filled the copper kettle and one or two large containers with water, heating them over a wood fire. We separated the hogs to be slaughtered from the others, then chased the victims and prodded them to their place of execution. Dad downed them with a .22 caliber bullet to the brain. He tied short ropes to the hind legs and hoisted the hog up quickly on a high wooden tripod, then slit its throat so the animal could bleed. It was critical to get the blood out of the animal quickly so it wouldn't taint the meat. Once the hog was dead and bled, several men lowered the carcass into a large barrel of scalding hot water until the hair became soft enough to be removed with a round hog scraper, a small circular sharpened piece of steel fastened to a short wooden handle.

Levi Sommers was in charge of the scalding process and when the time was right, he yelled, "That's enough, raise 'er up!" He then tested the skin with the scraper to see if the carcass was ready. Sometimes the men had to lower it into the hot water several times before the scalding was complete. They then laid the hog on a large table for scraping. It was a matter of pride to end up with a hairless, white scraped carcass that gleamed in the morning sun.

The men then hung the hog again, gutted and beheaded it. From the gut pile they removed the intestines, which the ladies emptied, washed, and cleaned to be used later for sausage casings. Dad stuck the head onto a fence post to cool. Most of that would become headcheese, except for the ears, which were to be boiled or pickled later. I loved the taste of the chewy ears, especially when served with applesauce. We also saved the stomach. Mother cleaned and filled the stomach lining with seasoned vegetables and baked it for a delicious meal. Pickled pigs' feet were another delicacy.

The men removed the outer layer of skin and fat and we kids were given the task of cutting them into small pieces. We threw them into a rendering pot, where they cooked until the lard separated out, leaving a clear hot liquid. The solid remains, called cracklings, were removed and placed in a pot to cool. Everyone helped themselves to these tasty tidbits. Mom and we kids then dipped out the thick liquid, filtered it, and stored it in large containers to be used for cooking. Everything was greasy and full of saturated fats, but we, having never heard of cholesterol, consumed it with delight.

While some of us were rendering the lard, others were grinding up the pork. This was basically the meat left over after the bacon sides, hams, and loins were removed. When Levi had a tub full of meat, he added salt, pepper, and other seasonings to make the sausage. The women slipped the cleaned intestines over the outside of the sausage press spout. Dad or Levi cranked the press and slowly forced the sausage into the casings. Soon huge coils of sausage lay on the table. Mother took short strings and tied part of the sausage into links. The sausage was then canned or smoked; either way it was tasty.

"Time for schnitz pie!" Mother would suddenly announce, and

everything came to a screeching halt. We all helped ourselves to one or two slices of the delicious dried apple pies. The men discussed the price of corn, hogs, and milk, the ladies exchanged the latest gossip in the neighborhood, and we kids played.

When the break was over, everyone got back to his assigned tasks. The men hung the sausages and bacon sides in the smokehouse. The women prepared the hams by inserting a syringe needle into the large veins and filling them with a curing material. They rubbed the outside of the hams with a heavy solution of salt, pepper, brown sugar, and saltpeter, and placed them in the smokehouse. There the meat would hang for days or weeks as the low cold smoke gradually cured them. The dark smokehouse smelled of smoke and cured meat for months.

By late evening the whole hog butchering process was done. We enjoyed the bacon and hams for a few months but there was never enough to last for a year. When these cured meats were gone, we did without them until the next hog butchering. That was true of most of our food items. After the fresh garden vegetables and fruits were no longer available we made do with canned stuff. We never bought things from the store to supplement a diminished supply but we always had plenty to eat.

We consumed a lot of food during the course of a year. Eventually there were nine of us and since we worked hard physically and ate three large meals a day, we needed a lot of victuals to satisfy our appetites. Basically the food was all organically grown, but we had never heard that phrase. To us it was homegrown and delicious.

8

THE DEPRESSION

The decade after World War I was a period of prosperity and growth in the United States. Nearly everyone had a job and money. "Let the good times roll," people would say, and it seemed they would roll on forever.

It was in these optimistic times that my father bought the farm in 1920. He was only twenty-three and must have felt pride in purchasing a farm at such a young age. He was still single, but he and my mother planned to be married in the fall.

My dad had been orphaned at the age of ten when his father died from blood poisoning after being bitten by a rat. His mother had died when Dad was two years old, so my father went to live with his older sister Mary and her husband. Dad apparently had saved some money by the time he became an adult and he had also inherited from his father's estate. With these savings he made the down payment on the farm and purchased a few horses, livestock, and some machinery. He paid $250 an acre for our seventy-eight-acre farm. That was a lot of money in 1920, but as I often heard him say later, "Everone thot da goot prices for crops and livestock vood go on forefer."

The 1920s were good to my parents. They not only acquired a farm but also became parents to five children by 1930. This was a good start toward a large family, so important to an Amish farm couple. The farm had good black soil and became more productive as Dad applied his Amish farming skills. By rotating crops and spreading lots of animal wastes on the fields as fertilizer, the crop yields increased. It appeared this would be a farm that would remain in the Troyer family for many generations.

At first farm products such as corn, wheat, soybeans, hogs, milk, and eggs brought good prices and the payments on the farm loan were easily made. My folks even had surplus money to buy additional farm tools and household items. Then, in 1929, with little warning, the bottom dropped out of the U.S. economy. Farm products were now worth a fraction of what they had been only a few months before. Suddenly cash was hard to acquire and my parents had a difficult time making payments on the farm loan. The $250 an acre my father had paid for the farm now seemed an atrocious price. My parents hated to give up the farm and continued to save every dollar to make the payments, hoping the Depression would ease. They gradually went deeper and deeper in debt.

This must have been a traumatic time for them as they saw their dreams of the future shattering—a future that had looked so bright when they married.

There came a time when there was no money to make the payments, and my parents lost the farm. It would be an experience that would stay with them the rest of their lives. Future economic decisions were always colored by the phrase "…until the next Depression hits."

I was only four years old when the Depression began, but I soon learned that my folks had little cash on hand. We were taught that every penny counted and, if we ever got one, it was immediately put in our piggy bank for the future.

When my parents lost the farm, they had already paid $7,500 of the nearly $20,000 loan. Now they were forced to become renters of the land they had once owned. The heirs to the farm, Omar and Carolyn Smith, gave my folks all the breaks they could, but even so my parents had trouble earning enough to pay the rent and buy a few basics. They thought highly of the Smiths, whom they considered fair and honest, and eventually named two of their children after them.

The Smiths urged my parents to re-purchase the farm when it was again put up for sale in 1934 for a total of $4,600 ($60 per acre), but they had no way of earning enough money to make the payments, even though they were lower.

We were not the only family to be hit hard by the Depression. Many others were losing their farms. Some farmers were forced to sell their livestock and implements and move into town, where they competed for the few low-paying jobs available.

Those of us who managed to stay on the farm, however, were lucky in many respects. We could grow our own food and had plenty to eat. We didn't consider ourselves poor because we had little cash, for all our neighbors had the same financial problems. Our situation was quite different from many people in the cities who could not grow their own food and didn't have enough money to purchase it. The newspapers published many graphic pictures of people standing in long soup lines.

When President Roosevelt took office in 1933, he signed into law the Works Project Administration, as part of the New Deal, to put people back to work. I still remember the long lines of WPA workers that toiled along rural roadsides, digging and cleaning the ditches with pick and shovel to earn $2 a day. These meager wages provided many people essential funds so they could buy food for their families instead of standing in the soup lines. Other citizens became homeless. We occasionally got tramps at our house who had ridden the rails to McGrawsville, then gotten off the train and visited various farms in hopes of a meal. Mother was often apprehensive about strangers with their ragged clothes and their few belongings slung over their shoulders in a sack, but she always sent them on their way with something to eat. Occasionally, if they arrived late in the evening, Dad let them sleep in the barn for the night.

I still remember one occasion when I almost injured a visiting tramp. I went to the barn early in the morning to pitch hay to the horses. I stuck my pitchfork into a pile of hay and suddenly a voice cried out, "Don't stick me! Don't stick me!" I jumped back in horror and watched as the stack of hay suddenly moved and a tramp in ragged clothes emerged from the pile. Dad had forgotten to tell me that he had given the man permission to sleep in the barn that night.

Christmas gifts were limited in those years. Like all children, we hoped for a few toys, but we usually received only essential items such as homemade sweaters, coats, and shoes. We tried to pretend handmade coats and a pair of newly darned socks were exactly what we wanted. I doubt we fooled our parents, since we didn't exactly shriek with delight when we unwrapped the mended clothes. Mother always made lots of candies for Christmas, which we did relish and looked forward to with much anticipation. We were especially fond of her chocolate drops, and she had to make several hundred to satisfy our sweet tooths.

During the Depression years, Mother often butchered some of our chickens and churned extra butter; then on Saturdays she peddled them through various neighborhoods in Kokomo. Selling from door to door brought more cash than selling through the regular farm markets.

The Depression may have also limited the size of our family. Mother had given birth about every two years from 1921, when Almeda was born, to 1930 when my youngest sister Miriam arrived. At the beginning of the Depression, childbearing suddenly ceased. Supposedly, the Amish didn't practice birth control, but apparently the policy was somewhat altered by my folks during those tough times. They didn't resume expanding the family until 1935 when my brother Omar was born, followed by Philip in 1937. That completed their family of four boys and three girls.

Money problems caused by the Depression were compounded by another event that eventually led to another huge change in our lives. At the beginning of the Depression, my Mom's mother Grandma Marner died, the only grandparent that I ever knew. Soon after her death, her farm was sold and the bishop of our Amish church was made the administrator of the estate. Mother was one of only two children, and should have received a fair sum of money from the proceeds, but apparently she got very little. Considerable bitterness developed between my parents and the leaders of the church over this financial situation. I was too young to know of the details, but in later years I asked about the particulars. Mother's only reply was, "The bishop turned crooked."

As the feud continued between my parents and the hierarchy of the Amish church, we started missing Sunday services. The episode would set my folks to thinking the unthinkable—the possibility of leaving the Amish church.

9

WE BECOME MENNONITES

Because of the conflict between my folks and the Amish bishop, we had not attended a preaching service for over a month. One Sunday morning I overheard my parents discussing the situation. They both agreed that they must start attending church somewhere for the sake of us children, but I never heard enough of the conversation to hear where we might go. I was concerned because I enjoyed my Amish friends who talked Pennsylvania Dutch and dressed like I did.

That morning Mom told us to get dressed in our Sunday best, then we piled into the buggy. My folks seemed more somber than usual. When we reached the end of the lane, Dad turned the horses south. We kids were surprised to be going in the opposite direction of the main stream of buggies. Almeda finally asked, "Where are we goin'?"

"Yes, where are we goin'?" several of us chimed in.

There was silence for a minute, then Mother replied, "We are goin' to the Mennonite church today."

"The Mennonite church! We won't know anybody there," Joel said.

"You'll know quite a few kids," Mother said, and she started naming some of the kids we knew in the Clay-Miami school we attended.

The Mennonite church was a large white building that stood at the intersection of two county roads. The parking lot was full of cars when we arrived, so Dad drove the horses to the back of the lot and tied Ben and Minor to a fence post. We got out of the buggy and walked to the front of the church. Dad and we boys went into the cloakroom on the left as Mom and our sisters went right. The Mennonites, like the Amish, also segregated by gender for services. The spacious church held about three hundred people. Our parents knew many members, and after we had hung our big black hats in the cloakroom, Dad started talking to a friend who suggested where we could sit. Joel and I followed him up the aisle and we sat down on one of the long benches. As I scooted into my seat, I thought, Boy, these sure are comfortable.

The benches had backs and curved seats that fit my bottom instead of the hard, flat, backless benches the Amish used. Soon a man got up in front and started speaking in English. For the first time I could understand the church service.

The Amish and Mennonites are similar in many ways. Like the Amish, the Mennonites were part of the Anabaptist movement that started in Europe in the 1500s.

They also do not believe in infant baptism and are pacifists, refusing to participate in war or other types of violence.

Major differences do exist, however. The Mennonites use cars, tractors, electricity, telephones, and nearly all other modern conveniences. They do not practice shunning nor ban higher education. The Mennonites, in fact, administer several colleges in the United States.

Different Mennonite groups vary on how they dress, but in this church many members tended to dress on the plain side. Some of the men had straight collars on their coats while others donned neckties. All men wore regular pants with a zippered or buttoned fly in front. A few of the men had beards, but they were not required. Women wore rather plain dresses but were allowed patterned colors, unlike the strictly solid-colored dresses of the Amish. Some even flaunted short sleeves, though I do remember later when Bishop Ansen Horner stood at the pulpit and admonished the ladies not to wear short sleeves, showing their bare arms, while serving people at a church social. All women wore prayer caps. Some had large ones that covered their head like their Amish counterparts, but many wore tiny caps on the back of their heads that had to be pinned so they wouldn't fall off. Women were not allowed to cut their hair, but many of the younger women, wanting to appear sophisticated, rolled their hair up to look more elegant. This hairstyle was referred to as the Mennonite roll.

The leader in front of the church made a few remarks, and then the congregation sang several hymns in English. These were snappy tunes compared to the long, drawn out hymns of the Amish. After attending church awhile, I soon sang with gusto, *"When the roll is called up yonder, I'll be there,"* and *"At the cross, at the cross, where I first saw the light."*

Joel and I were led downstairs to a Sunday School class for boys our age. The class was conducted in English and we were encouraged to participate. I was quite bashful, and when the teacher asked me a question, I only shook my head yes or no. When Sunday School was over, we filed back upstairs and listened to the English sermon that was only forty minutes long. I was elated that I could understand the sermon, but it also got boring after a while.

One of the biggest advantages of the Mennonite service was that it lasted only two-and-a-half hours compared to the four-hour Amish marathon. Going downstairs to Sunday School, and then walking back upstairs also helped keep away the boredom I had experienced in the Amish church. We didn't get cookies during the service, however, or stay for a meal afterward where I could dip apple butter bread into a cup of coffee. Mom made up for the loss of the after preachin' meal by making Sunday dinner at home our biggest and best meal of the week with lots of pies and other desserts.

After attending the new church for a couple of months, my parents joined and officially became Mennonites. Of course, the Amish bishop called for shunning us, but many people ignored the directive; we continued to visit with some of our Amish neighbors and relatives.

Despite the difference in churches, my parents did not make any drastic changes in their lifestyles for some time. We continued to drive the horse and buggy. Dad kept his beard and many of his Amish clothes; Mom also wore her plain clothes. But gradually changes happened. Before long Mother bought us boys store-bought denim pants that had a fly in front instead of the Amish-style flap. I was beginning to look like the 'English' kids in school. I liked dressing like most kids and noticed I wasn't teased about my clothes any more. Soon Mom quit wearing her big bonnet and cape. She started making my sisters more modern dresses and gave Joel and me regular haircuts. We could now see our ears when we looked in a mirror.

I made a lot of friends in church and started looking forward to Sundays. But although the Mennonite morning service was much shorter than the Amish one, all good Mennonites also went to church on Sunday evening. So after milking and the evening chores, we got dressed up and went to church again. And then there was prayer meeting in the middle of the week. I groaned at that one, but my folks were adamant that we attend all three services. There was also a summer Bible school that all children had to attend for two weeks. I didn't mind that too much because it was held in the hot summer days, and I got out of some monotonous farm work, such as hoeing weeds, repairing fences, and cleaning out the chicken houses. The Mennonites also held several revival meetings about twice a year that lasted for a week.

I complained to my mother one day that I thought we were spending too much time going to church. "It'll do you good, and when you git older you'll understand," was her curt reply.

There was a lot of hellfire and brimstone preaching at the revival meetings. Some preachers roared when they predicted, "The end of the world is about to come and you better be ready!"

It scared me to death. I wanted to be ready and when I got home and went to bed, I pulled the covers over my head, shaking and praying, "Lord, don't let the end come tonight!"

The Mennonites encouraged young children to participate in all religious activities. At special Sunday evening meetings, kids were asked to recite Bible verses in front of the church. It was often a traumatic experience for us shy kids. The first time I was asked to participate, I memorized Psalm 100. My mother drilled me all week. I practiced reciting the verses when I was milking, while pitching down hay, when I was walking to school, and lying in my bed at night, until I had it down pat. When I finally stood in front of the church, I was sweaty and tense. My knees were knocking and my hands shook. But when I opened my mouth to speak, nothing came out. I stared at the ceiling and slipped my hands in and out of my pockets. I tried to speak several times, while the crowd sat hushed. I just couldn't get any words to come out of my mouth. Finally, Mrs. Miller said, "Make a joyful shout...," to get me started. I blurted out the verses in staccato fashion and ran back to my seat.

The next boy got up and faced the crowd. He stood ramrod straight for a few moments, waiting for silence, then in a loud voice said, "Jesus wept," and sat down.

I thought to myself, "Wow! 'Jesus wept!' Why didn't I think of that?"

"Yes, that's nice, Johnny," said Mrs. Miller. "That is the shortest verse in the Bible."

I suggested to my mother that I recite the "Jesus wept" verse the next time, but she said that was too easy.

Sometimes we participated by answering questions. One Sunday they got all of us kids in front of the church, then Mrs. Zook asked, "Now who can name a sin?"

A whole bunch of hands shot up.

Pointing to David, she said, "O.K., David."

"Smoking."

"Yes, smoking's bad," Mrs. Zook said.
Encouraged by David's success, other kids started reeling off other sins.
"Drinking."
"Going to the movies."
"Sayin' cuss words."
"Killin'."
"Adultery."
"Stealin'."

Man! There were all kinds of sinful things, some I had never heard of. Then my little sister Miriam's hand went up. Let me explain that Miriam had a habit of intently staring at strangers. For us pious people that wasn't considered polite. If you wanted to look at people, you sort of turned your head away and looked out of the corner of your eye, so they didn't notice. We had reminded little Miriam several times not to stare directly at people.

"Yes, Miriam, can you name a bad sin?" asked Mrs. Zook.

"Standing and staring!" Miriam answered in a loud voice.

Mrs. Zook about dropped her Bible. A low chuckle rippled through the congregation. "Yes, that's not nice," she finally said.

When I started noticing the young girls across the aisle a few years later, I enjoyed going to church a lot more. Soon I was leaning forward to exchange smiles with Miriam Sommers. It made the service go a lot faster. We even traded school pictures. Neither was brave enough to give the picture directly to the other. My sister Sylvia was the go-between, passing the photos at our request. Then some old biddy in church noticed our little exchanges. She told my mother it was not the thing to do in church. Mom admonished me about my hidden romance. I was floored. I had no idea she knew. I was pretty upset about the episode, especially since I had to quit looking at Miriam so often. It sure took the fun out of church.

Once my parents started attending the Mennonite services on a regular basis, I think they preferred them to the Amish services. Mom was a little on the liberal side for an Amish woman, and I knew Dad had had a wild side to him when he was young. We kids once found some photos in the attic of Dad smoking a cigarette and playing an accordion with a group of young Amish. That was in his *rumspringa* (running around) days, before he joined the Amish church. He kept the accordion in spite of the ban on musical instruments. When I was about six, he started teaching me a few tunes. One day, as he was giving me instructions, the Amish preacher drove up the lane in a buggy. Dad quickly grabbed the accordion, ran upstairs and hid it in the closet. "Now don't tell da preacher," he whispered to me before the preacher came inside.

In many ways becoming Mennonites was a small adjustment, but it would open up larger changes for our family in the future.

*Will Troyer at 10 years of age,
after his family became Mennonites
and no longer wore Amish clothes*

10

DAD BUYS A CAR

One evening at the supper table Dad announced that he and Mother were going to Peru the next day to buy a car. "A car! A car!" several of us kids yelled.

It was like announcing they were taking us around the world, a near financial impossibility. After my parents joined the Mennonites, they talked about someday owning a car, but we had no idea it would be so soon. We knew our folks had little money and didn't think they could afford a car until they got rich. During the Depression we always talked about getting rich someday.

"Can you drive, Dad?" someone asked.

"No. But Treat Morton is gonna teach me," Dad said.

Then he laid out the plans. Treat would pick up Mom and Dad in the morning after the chores and take them to Peru to look for a car. Miriam, who wasn't in school yet at age four, would stay with our neighbor Mary Ann. We older kids were instructed to do the milking and the rest of the chores when we got home from school, because it might be late when they got home.

It was in the fall of 1934, and I had just turned nine, Joel was eleven, Almeda thirteen, and Sylvia seven. Together we were capable of doing about anything on the farm and my parents had complete confidence in us.

I could hardly sleep that night thinking about the car. Boy, that is sure going to be something, driving around the neighborhood and showing off our car, I fancied.

The next day, school seemed to go on forever. I thought about telling a couple of my Amish buddies that my folks were going to buy a car but decided not to. Lately, several of them had been calling me "Willard the Mennonite" as a way of poking fun at me. Now, I was not only different from my 'English' friends, but also different from the

Amish in their eyes. I didn't seem to fit in with either group.

We hurried to finish our chores after school, then Joel and I ran out to the lane and sat on the fence watching for our parent's return. We waited anxiously for nearly an hour before I saw a car approach.

"I'll bet that's them!" I yelled and stood on top of the fence to get a better view. But excitement turned to disappointment when Joel recognized it as a neighbor's car.

I glumly sat back down.

Just before dark a strange car approached from the north. "I wonder if that could be them," Joel said.

"Yeah! Yeah! I'll bet that's Mom and Dad!" I shouted.

About then, the car turned into the lane.

"Go tell the girls! Go tell the girls!" Joel yelled at me.

I ran into the house shouting, "They're comin'! They're comin'!"

Almeda and Sylvia, who had been preparing supper, ripped off their aprons and the three of us raced out the door. We all climbed up on the fence and watched the black shiny car slowly chug up our lane, until finally it was right in front of us.

What a beautiful car! I couldn't believe my eyes. Knowing my parents didn't have much money, I'd expected them to buy one of those high-topped Model T cars that were still driven by many people. But this was a sleek modern-looking car. I was overwhelmed with what I saw. Joel shouted breathlessly, "I think it's a Model A Ford!"

Dad was in the driver's seat, gripping the steering wheel with both hands, his big black hat sitting jauntily atop his head. Mom and little Miriam were in the back seat, smiling and waving. Treat Morton sat next to Dad, directing the driving. They continued to the barnyard while we kids ran behind.

After Dad got the car stopped, they sat in it for a few minutes while Treat instructed Dad on how to shut off the engine. We kids walked around the vehicle admiring the sleek sides and running our hands over the smooth metal body, still not convinced it was real.

Finally our parents got out of the automobile. Dad, proud as a peacock, strutted around the car. Mom was exhilarated and all smiles. "Well, what do you children think of this fancy machine?" she asked.

"It's a 1930 Model A Ford."

"Boy, it's shiny."

"It's so big."

"It looks new."

"Look at the fancy seats!"

"Can we get in?" I asked.

It looked so brand spanking clean and new that I was afraid Dad would say no.

"Go ahead, but don't put your dirty feet on da seats," Dad said.

All five kids jumped in the back, clamoring and struggling to fit in. Then Joel and I climbed over the top into the front seat. Soon we were all fighting to sit behind the wheel and pretend we were steering it down the road. Boy, this was the most excitement since the horse race going to Amish preaching.

After we all had our turn at pretend driving, Mom said, "Now that's enough for tonight, kids. Let's go in the house and see what Almeda fixed for supper."

We gathered around the supper table asking more questions about the car. How much did it cost? How fast does it go? Does it start easy? Do you have to crank it? Does it take a lot of gas?

The next morning at breakfast Dad announced he was going to drive the car in the bean field. The soybeans had already been harvested. The ground was flat and dry, an ideal place to practice driving. It was Saturday and we didn't have school. "Can we go? Can we go?" we begged.

Dad grinned, which we took for a yes, and before he could reply we were out the door running for the car. There was plenty of room, but we all wanted to sit in the front seat and fought to get in. Almeda and Joel beat me to the seat and I found myself sitting on Almeda's lap, much to my disgust. I grudgingly moved to the back. When our father arrived, he told everyone to get in the back, because he didn't want us in the way when he was learning to drive. I smiled gleefully.

Dad slipped behind the wheel, then got out Treat Morton's instructions. "Let's see now…turn on da switch, advance da spark…"

He stepped on the starter. *Vroom, vroom, vroom.* The starter groaned but nothing happened. We were silent and tense, waiting for the motor to start. Then *Bang*! The engine backfired. We jumped like grasshoppers, then howled with laughter.

"Did you hear that? Did you hear that?" Joel shouted.

Then he whispered to me, "I think it farted." We both giggled at his little joke, but Almeda overheard it.

"Dad, the boys are talkin' dirty."

"Now, you boys cut dat out or I'll wash your mout' out with soap n' water."

Apparently Dad had advanced the spark too much. He read the instructions again, then stepped on the starter. This time the engine caught and the motor began racing. In his excitement our father had rammed the accelerator to the floor.

"Let's go! Let's go!" one of us shouted.

"Now ya kids be quiet or I'll make ya git out," he said.

When Dad let out the clutch, the Model A jumped forward, spilling us kids against the back of the seat. Dad grabbed the steering wheel with both hands and yelled "Whooooa!" Fortunately the gate to the bean field was open. The car shot through the narrow opening, barely missing a post. We raced down the field, bouncing over ruts for a few moments before Dad remembered to lift his foot off the accelerator. He headed for the center of the field, then brought the car to a stop. Dad was thirty-eight years old and had been an Amishman all his life. He wanted to pull on the steering wheel like he pulled on the lines to turn a team of horses.

We kids watched every move. "Now *sitzen*. I'm gonna take off agin."

He shifted into first gear, let out the clutch, and the car lurched forward. Then he shifted again and stepped on the gas. The car flew down the bean field as the speedometer needle climbed to 25 mph. Suddenly we became silent with fright for none of us had ever traveled at such a high speed in a field. Slowly Dad turned the car in a big circle, then practiced sudden turns to the left and right, which threw us kids from one side of the back seat to the other until we were all in a heap. We became used to the wild ride and were soon laughing and shouting for more.

"Go, Dad, go!" Joel yelled.

Dad complied. Several of us tried to stand up, but a sudden turn threw us on top of each other again.

"Faster, faster!" we screamed.

We must have got Dad in a racing mood, because the Model A circled around the field recklessly. As we approached the far end of the bean field, near the cattle pasture, the cows saw us coming, stuck their tails in the air and ran from the monster.

"Look at the cows! Look at 'em run!"

Dad soon steered the automobile back to the center of the field and stopped, shifted into reverse…forward, reverse, forward, reverse…time and again until he had the gear shifting down pat. After an hour of practicing, he drove back to the barn and parked. He was driving more smoothly now and was convinced he had mastered this mechanical horse.

We all got out of the Model A and again ran our hands over the smooth sides that were now covered with dust from the bean field. Then Dad said to Almeda, "Go git yer Mom, ve're gonna go ta McGrawsville."

We jumped up and down with joy, screaming and yelling in anticipation of a ride on the road.

Mom and little Miriam got in the front seat with Dad and the rest of us piled in the rear. As Dad started the car and shifted it into gear, he explained each step to Mom as she also wanted to learn to drive. We putt-putted out the lane onto the road. When we went by the Sommers and Mortons, Dad honked the horn and we kids leaned out the windows and waved. When we passed our Amish neighbors, Dad told us not to wave. He didn't want to alienate them.

Dad stepped on the gas until the speedometer indicated 35 mph. What speed! The wind whistled through the back windows and sent our hair flying as we screamed with delight. Mom and Dad were both laughing at our excitement. It was the fastest any of us kids had ever traveled. When we got to McGrawsville, Dad stopped in front of the store and we all went in for an all-day candy sucker to celebrate getting the Model A Ford.

"So you bought a car," the store manager said.

"Ja, I did." Dad grinned.

"How is the driving going?"

"O.K., O.K.," Dad said. "It's faster dan drivin' a buggy."

Soon all the neighbors knew the Troyers had bought a car. Mary Ann got on the telephone and spread the news that the Troyers bought a shiny black Model A ford. Even without phones the Amish soon knew about the car.

The next day we went to church in the new auto. Dad sat in the front passenger seat and instructed Mom. It was the blind leading the blind, but there wasn't much traffic on the rural gravel roads and we got there without incident.

Mom soon became a better driver than Dad. He was always looking at the neighbors' crops instead of watching the road. Consequently the Model A did a lot of weaving back and forth as it putted down the country roads when Dad was at the wheel.

Several years later, while he was driving and intently looking at a neighbor's cornfield, he ran right smack over George Ehrman's mailbox. Now, George had had his mailbox run over several times and had got tired of repairing the broken post, so he bolted a piece of heavy flat steel along the side of the post. When Dad hit it, the steel plate sliced through the running board and ripped a slit in the side of the car. Dad not only had to fix Ehrman's mailbox, he also spent considerable time repairing the car until it looked almost new.

To Dad, a good driver was one who drove slowly, and he vowed to never go over 40 mph. One morning as we were going to church at about 35 mph, we got behind an old man who was wheeling along at 20 mph. Dad never passed him.

"Boy, he issa goot driver," our father said several times, while we kids fidgeted in the back seat.

We followed the slow driver for two miles. When he came to Highway 31, a busy Indiana state road, the good driver continued past the big red "STOP" sign and across the highway at the same steady 20 mph. Everyone was silent for a moment.

"Yeah, Dad, he sure is a good driver," I mimicked.

Everyone snickered, but my father never said a word, realizing his lesson had flopped.

As the years went by and we kids learned to drive, our parents would warn us, "Now, don't go over 40." For a long time the Model A never saw any fast speeds until Joel and I were given solo privileges. It was then I found the 40 mph Model A could do better than 60!

Like a lot of American families in the early automotive age, the car changed our lives. We were no longer confined to our small neighborhood. We went to town more often, and traveled a lot farther to shop and visit. We started purchasing things we had formerly made or raised at home, and we became less dependent upon our neighbors. It was the beginning of a big social change that didn't become apparent to us until many years later.

II

WE MOVE

Our McGrawsville farm was sold to an Amish couple in the fall of 1934. Our parents still did not have enough money to buy one of their own, so they spent the latter part of that year looking at farms for rent. They wanted to find one within the Mennonite-Amish community but couldn't find anything suitable. They settled for a 160-acre farm five miles west of Kokomo near Wildcat Creek in Clay Township, Howard County. It was one of the early homesteads developed in Clay Township prior to the Civil War and was called the Smith Farm, after H.W. Smith, the original owner. The farm was fifteen miles from our Mennonite church, but with the new automobile they thought they could commute to the thrice-weekly services. We moved early in 1935.

Access to our new home was a picturesque winding road that paralleled Wildcat Creek. The area had numerous hardwood groves, small streams, and many gullies and hills, far different from the flat countryside of our McGrawsville neighborhood.

The farm buildings sat a quarter-mile back from Wildcat Creek Road. Our new house was a large two-story brick building surrounded by huge maple trees, long branches caressing the roof during a brisk breeze. The downstairs had two bedrooms, a living room, dining room, and kitchen, all graced by twelve-foot ceilings. A long winding stairway with a curved railing led upstairs. The first time I saw the railing, the temptation was too great. I straddled it at the top, whooped, "Here I come!" and slid to the bottom.

"Boy, this is gonna be fun!" I called to Mom. The railing ride became a favorite pastime for us kids.

The upstairs had two more bedrooms, an attic, and a balcony that looked out over the front yard and nearby woods. A smokehouse and a well house were near the rear of our new home. Two barns and a combination corn crib/implement shed sat west of the house. A chicken house at the edge of the orchard to the north completed the complex.

The buildings had been a bit neglected. The barns were weatherworn and unpainted. During an earlier visit to the farm, my mother walked around the outside of the house. In the rear was a huge pile of tin cans she looked at with fury.

"Any woman too lazy to can and buys store-bought stuff is not fit to be a farm wife! What a waste of money! And to dump everything in the yard! I hope I never meet her. If I do, I'll give her a piece of my mind!" She stuck her nose in the air and stepped around the pile of cans.

Forty acres of woods broken into two groves squeezed up to the edge of the buildings on the east and west sides. A small stream flowed through the woods, meandered past the barns, crossed under a bridge in the lane, and continued to Wildcat Creek, three-quarters of a mile away.

The woods were filled with hickory, walnut, beech, elm, maple, oak, and chestnut trees. A seven-acre tract in the northwestern corner of the woods had been cut over and now harbored a dense thicket of saplings. We sometimes got disoriented in this section and had to walk in widening circles to find our way out. During spring, the leafy ground was covered with a carpet of wildflowers. We often filled our straw hats with morel mushrooms and took them home, a delicacy our mother appreciated. The eastern section of the woods had numerous maple trees, and Dad permitted our neighbor Hugh Smith to tap them each spring for his sugaring business. Joel and I frequently filled our stomachs from the sap buckets while searching for birds and other wildlife. An old rail fence separated the orchard from the west woods and served as a runway for fox and pine squirrels.

The woods, orchard, stream, fields, and farm buildings provided a diverse habitat for wildlife. Cardinals, robins, bluebirds, barn swallows, blue jays, house wrens, orioles, and a variety of sparrows and warblers congregated in the area. We were serenaded with bird songs every dawn in spring and summer. Redheaded woodpeckers and flickers drummed their rat-a-tat-tat rhythms on dead snags. In the deep woods and thickets my brother and I found nests of brown thrashers, catbirds, buntings, sparrows, and thrushes. The wily crows hid their nests in the tall trees, but Joel and I searched them out. We climbed up to steal their eggs because our father offered us a penny an egg to reduce the crow population, which decimated the newly planted cornfields.

The numerous old-growth hickory, walnut, and beech trees provided plenty of denning sites for fox squirrels that ran up the trunks and nimbly jumped from limb to limb. A few raccoons, opossum, and an occasional weasel traveled the creek banks. In winter we sometimes found fox tracks in the snow. Cottontails thrived in the bushy fencerows and dense grain fields.

This farm was paradise to a budding naturalist like myself. At every chance I sneaked off to watch the wildlife. When summer came, we kids found an abundance of crayfish, minnows, frogs, tadpoles, turtles, water striders, and other aquatic creatures in the little brook. We spent many hours wading barefoot through the creek in search of little wiggly things. In the spring, with our cane poles, Joel and I occasionally caught small fish to eat, which we called shiners.

Even in the house we lived close to nature. Screech owls often sat in trees outside our bedroom window and sounded loud quavering calls in the middle of the night that sent shivers up our spines. Joel and I shared an upstairs bedroom, and one morning before daylight, we were awakened by something jumping on our bed. We were frightened and pulled the bed covers over our heads. We could hear the creature scurrying around the room and screamed to Dad for help.

"It's a monster!" I shrieked.

Finally Dad came upstairs with a lantern in one hand and a broom in the other. "Git it, Dad! Git it!" we yelled.

About then, the monster jumped from the ceiling to the foot of our bed again. Dad swung the broom wildly several times and finally connected, knocking the animal against the far wall and crippling the poor creature. "Got it!" he yelled and crushed it with his shoe.

Joel and I finally looked out from under the blankets and saw Dad standing there holding a dead flying squirrel by the tail. "I thought it was bigger than that," I mumbled. Joel had thought it was a big rat.

One Sunday morning there was a commotion in the hen house. "Somethin' is after the chickens!" Mom yelled and rushed out the door. Soon she came racing back.

"Where's the gun?"

Joel ran to the basement and returned with the .22 rifle. "Here're the shells," he said as he handed her the gun.

Mom ran out again and we boys started to follow. "Stay back," she said. "It's a weasel and I'm gonna shoot it." She disappeared into the chicken house.

Pretty soon we heard a bang! bang!, then silence. Mother stepped out holding the dead weasel by the tail. "Look at this little monster!" she shouted. "It killed three chickens."

The weasel had squeezed through a tiny hole in the chicken house and filled its stomach with chicken blood until it was too fat to get back out.

I continued using the Arm & Hammer colored cards to identify birds but I lacked cards for numerous species. My mother also enjoyed bird watching and encouraged my interest. One day while shopping in Kokomo, she noticed a thick bird book for sale and told me about it. On her next trip to town I went with Mom, and the store clerk let me look through the book. It was the first edition of *The Birds of America*, written by the top ornithologists of the day. As I turned the pages and scanned the pictures, my eyes were wide with wonder. I recognized a number of birds that I had been unable to identify previously. I coveted the book, but it cost $3.95, a prohibitive price. I really wanted that book. Mother saw the burning desire in my eyes.

"Well, maybe if you save your pennies, you can buy it someday."

All the way home I thought about the book. When we got to the house I ran to my room, drained out my piggy bank, and counted the coins. I was exactly one dollar short. I thought of nothing but the bird book all week and let Mom know that I really wanted it. Several days later, she said, "I'll lend you a dollar and you can pay me back later."

I was astounded, as our parents never gave us kids spending money. I gave her all the money in my piggy bank and the next week, when she went to town, she returned with the book. I paged through it endlessly and by the time I was twelve, I knew almost every bird that lived in our woods.

I still have the book today. Though the pages are a bit frayed, on the inside cover remains my mother's simple handwritten inscription: *Willard Troyer, age 11, December 28, 1936.* It brings back many memories.

12

A NEW SCHOOL

The first Monday after we moved to the Smith farm, Mother made sure we had on clean clothes, then sent us to the end of the lane to wait for the school bus. I dreaded going to a new school where everyone would be a stranger. The four of us—Almeda, Joel, Sylvia, and I—waited reluctantly. My stomach churned. Would the new kids tease me? Would I make any new friends? Why did I have to go to school anyway? I threw rocks at a fence post, then kicked a nearby log repeatedly.

Joel, less concerned, chattered away. "I'll bet we'll meet new friends. It's gonna be fun to get to know some of the neighbors."

I thought he was crazy.

Finally, far to the west, the familiar yellow bus appeared. Almeda took one look and said, "Oh, oh, oh, I sure wish I didn't have to get on that bus. I'd just like to run back to the house. I won't know *anyone*!"

It was not a very reassuring statement coming from our older sister, the leader, but I felt the same way. As the bus came closer Joel said, "Look, it's almost full."

Everyone fell silent. When the bus stopped all eyes focused on us, the strange new kids. A few heads popped out of windows to get a better look. No Amish or Mennonites attended the school, so we must have looked a bit strange. My sisters wore plain-colored dresses and had their long hair braided, quite different from the short haircuts worn by most of the girls in the new school. Joel and I each had on a new pair of store-bought denim pants, but wore broad suspenders and handmade Amish shirts.

The door opened and Almeda led the way. The driver greeted us with a friendly "Hello," but the kids on the bus sat silently staring. There were several empty seats toward the rear, so we filed down the aisle and sat together. Heads turned to get another look at us. I felt like a freak in a circus and had to fight panicking and running off the bus. Instead, I sat silently with my siblings. To avoid the many piercing eyes we glumly stared out the windows or looked at our feet.

As the bus moved down the road, the chatter so common on a school bus full of kids gradually resumed. The bus driver followed the winding road along Wildcat Creek, stopping at various farms to pick up more kids, then crossed Highway 22 and drove north to the Clay Township school. The school sat in the middle of the township surrounded by farm fields, and all school bus routes led toward it like a hub.

*The Clay-Howard School
which I attended from Grade 3 through 12*

The schools in Howard County, like those in Miami County, had been consolidated around 1920. The Clay School, constructed in 1921, was a large two-story red brick building that accommodated about 225 students. Grades One through Six were housed in four rooms on the first floor, and Grades Seven through Twelve were on the top floor. The basement had a small gym, a home economics room, and a shop.

A number of buses had arrived in front of the school about the same time as ours. Students were pouring out of the vehicles, scurrying up the schoolhouse steps. It looked like absolute bedlam as we got off and followed the crowd. I had thought that my older sister would help me find my room, but I lost sight of her and my other siblings and was on my own, a lonely kid in a crowd of strangers.

A New School

I walked through the doors to see kids running upstairs and downstairs and disappearing into various classrooms. I stood still for a minute trying to find a sign that would lead me to the third grade room as kids flowed around me. None of them offered any help and I didn't expect any. A sign above the first door said Grade 6, so I turned left and followed the crowd down the long hallway. A student appeared on my left and gazed at me steadily. I got up a little courage and asked, "Can ya tell me where the third grade room is?"

"Sure, I'll show you." Then he led me down to the end of the hall.

It was the first friendly face I encountered and I was suddenly relieved of some anxieties. Later I would find out the student was Johnny Lovelace, a neighbor whom I got to know quite well in later years.

I walked through the third grade door and saw the teacher sitting at her desk in front of the room. Some kids were taking off their coats and putting them in lockers; others stared in my direction. I stood there hesitantly, not knowing what to do next. The teacher spotted me immediately, came over and introduced herself as Mrs. Donahue. "What's your name?" she asked.

"Willard Troyer."

"Come, Willard, and I'll show you to your desk."

She led me to a seat in the middle of the room, showed me where to hang my coat and where to put my lunch pail and books. There were kids everywhere, some sitting, some standing, and almost all talking. I didn't know at the moment that many of these students would become friends and classmates for the next nine years. I still remain close friends with many of them today.

A student with very clean well-pressed clothes, neatly combed hair, and shiny brown shoes walked over and stopped beside me. He propped his left foot on the edge of my seat and asked, "What's your name?"

I told him. He smiled and said, "I'm Bill Pearcy. This is a good school. You'll like it."

That little gesture suddenly relieved some of my nervousness. Bill would turn out to be the class clown, always joking, pulling tricks on the teachers, and keeping us laughing. He never applied himself to school textbooks but knew the intricate parts of a car and could fix every mechanical device made.

In a few minutes Mrs. Donahue stood up in front of the room, clapped her hands and said, "Everyone, take your seats."

Kids scurried for their desks and suddenly there was silence. Then she directed us to take out our reading books and assigned a chapter. She read the first page, then called on Joan Parker to read the next paragraph. As Joan completed her assignment, the teacher called on Esther, and then Eva Nellie. I was thinking nervously, Please, not me!

"Willard, would you read the next paragraph?" I suppose this was her way of evaluating my reading skills.

About half the students stared in my direction, no doubt wanting to know if the new kid was a dummy. It was so quiet you could have heard a pin drop. I caught my breath, swallowed, then started reading. When I finished, Mrs. Donahue said, "You read very well, Willard."

I felt a sense of pride and relief. This wasn't so bad after all.

The time passed quickly, and after a spelling lesson the teacher announced it was time for recess. Suddenly bedlam broke out as students jumped from their seats and started talking to friends. Others scurried for the door.

Bill Pearcy came to my desk accompanied by a boy with coal-black hair. "You wanna play kickball?"

"Sure." I nodded.

We grabbed our coats and headed outside. The dark-haired boy was Keith Wright, the smallest boy in the class. He had a great sense of humor. We became good friends and when together we often giggled so much that teachers automatically separated us to avoid class chaos.

Soon there were ten boys ready to play kickball. Among them was Ralph Deardorff, a dairy farmer's son; Gene Moss, who would become a professional well driller; Rex Dyar and David Haynes. David was tall and had on a pair of thick glasses that sat on the end of his nose as he peered over the top. He had a dry sense of humor and in later years he often let a real *bomber* slip in class. This made the rest of us ornery boys snicker incessantly. Then when silence returned, he turned his head and gave everyone an innocent grin. He became a principal, and I often wondered how he disciplined his students.

The kickball game got underway quickly. I had played the game before and was a fast runner for my age. With the encouragement of Bill and Keith I played intensively, trying to show everyone my athletic abilities and to help my team. When the bell rang, we raced back to our room and took our seats. I had lost some of my fear, for I could now put names to some of those strange faces and had a few friends.

The day went rather quickly with the mix of classes, recess, and lunch breaks. At the end of the day we filed out of the room and ran for the school buses. I recognized two students on my bus, so my fear of a busload of strangers had dissipated somewhat.

When we got off the bus and ran home, Mother immediately wanted to know how school had gone. "Oh, O.K." I muttered.

"What was your teacher's name?"

"Mrs. Donahue."

"Did you make any friends?"

I told her the names of a few of my new friends and how I had played kickball with them. Mother smiled. "Are there any girls in your class?"

"I guess so."

"Did you learn any of their names?"

"Nope."

"I'll bet the girls are just as nice as the boys," she said.

I looked at her and made a face. "You know I don't like girls, Mom."

She smiled, started walking away, then turned and said, "Now, you boys, change your clothes and go do the chores. The girls and I'll come out and help milk."

The next morning I didn't dread going to school as much, although I wasn't enthusiastic about it. I considered school a necessary evil that I couldn't escape.

The educational emphases at Clay School were reading, writing, math, history, and English. We were also required to take music. Poor Miss Stout struggled resolutely to drill a little culture into us rural kids. When we got older she forced us to listen to the Music Appreciation Hour on the radio. Her eyes sparkled as she stood in front of the class, "Now listen to the violins .... now the trombones!"

Her voice and animated hands vibrated with enthusiasm. I didn't appreciate classical music at all, but reluctantly became familiar with Mozart, Bach, Beethoven, and other composers. She must have succeeded in transferring some of her enthusiasm to us kids for I find myself listening to many of those classical pieces today.

Everything was geared to farm life, and we were expected to follow that occupation. The major course options in high school were agriculture and shop for the boys, home economics for the girls.

School started around September 1, after the busiest harvest season was over, and ended around the last week of April so that we could help with the spring planting. To compensate for the shorter school year, we did not get a spring vacation like the city kids did, and we had a shorter Christmas vacation.

Most of the teachers kept strict discipline in class, and if we strayed from the rules we were punished. Punishment might involve standing with our nose in a circle drawn on the blackboard, extra schoolwork, or just a reprimand in front of the class. If we did something real ornery, such as throw chalk at the teacher when her back was turned, the punishment was more severe.

One day in Mrs. Smith's class I took a piece of wadded paper and threw it across the room. She turned as I let go of the missile and caught me in the act. "Willard! You march right up here!" she yelled. "You can't get by with that kind of stuff in my class." I slowly slunk to the front of the room.

"Now lay your hands on top of the desk!" I obeyed, and she whacked me across the palms with her ruler unmercifully. It hurt, but I refused to show it.

"Now, get back to your seat and this afternoon at recess you will stay at your desk and study," she said.

Most parents approved of teacher punishment; the old edict was, "Spare the rod and spoil the child." In our home it was a standing policy that if we got a whipping at school, we would automatically receive another when we got home. I expected to get a whipping at home that day, but nobody tattled on me and I escaped the double punishment.

Mr. Hartman, our sixth grade teacher, demanded quiet classes and strict order. "Don't mess with Mr. Hartman" was the word passed when you got to his grade. I never tested his disciplinary tactics, but one day after performing some class work I didn't like, I walked into the boys' bathroom, grumbling. There were several boys in the room, and I boldly referred to Mr. Hartman as Mr. Fartman. John Daily, who was standing nearby, whooped loudly, "Mr. *Fartman*, ha, ha, ha!"

Mr. Hartman happened to be standing outside the bathroom and heard his name being taken in vain. He burst through the door, grabbed poor John, slammed him against the wall and gave him some good whacks across the face. I sneaked out the door and disappeared. I was afraid John would rat on me, but he never did.

My parents believed in strict discipline, and Mother kept a willow switch above the door for that purpose. As we got older, she couldn't hurt us boys physically, so she usually postponed the switching until evening when our father was home. He was capable of making it hurt, and I always dreaded waiting for my whipping.

As I recall, I received a whipping two or three times a week and was definitely number one in the family on that score. When I was quite small on our McGrawsville farm, my parents locked me in a very dark room in the cellar for serious misbehavior. I screamed and kicked the door until they let me out. I also developed a real fear of the dark that stayed with me for years.

After attending the new school for a few weeks, I started to really enjoy it. I made many new friends and was never teased about being Mennonite or Amish as I had been at Clay Miami. Later I read a lot of adventure and nature books, which improved my reading skills. When Mr. Gray, our history teacher, told us how the French explorers Joliet and Marquette traveled the Mississippi River and Daniel Boone roamed the wild frontier, he made it sound adventurous and I became a student of history. I also became involved in sports. These activities and my interests in a variety of subjects increased my desire to go to school. I liked the social life, and it was a good break from the routine farm work at home.

*My sophomore class at Clay-Howard School.
The numerous bib overalls reflect our rural upbringing.*

Top row from left:
   Mr. Schwartz, Glen Rogers, Ralph Deardorff, Gene Moss, John Packmeyer, Bill Pearcy, Keith Wright, Principal-Mr. Bowen.

Front row from left:
   Willard Troyer, David Haynes, Rex Dyar, Eva Erfcamp, Joan Parker, Wilma Harrison, Rosalee Bausom, Esther Graham.

13

BEAUTY THE PONY

My desire to have a pony never diminished, and I hadn't forgotten that my parents had promised a pony—s*omeday*. A few months after we moved to the Smith Farm, I again brought up the subject.

"Can we get a pony soon?" I asked one evening at the supper table. "If we had a pony, we could use it to bring in the cows."

"Yeah, and run errands to the neighbors," Joel added.

My sisters also wanted a pony and joined our request. Our combined enthusiasm was contagious. Dad finally said, "'Vell, I guess ve could use one. I'll look into it." We jumped up and down with glee.

From then on we kids talked about ponies all the time, and I started watching for pony ads in the Kokomo Tribune. Lots of horses were for sale but no ponies. Then several weeks later while scanning the Horse Column, I noticed: Shetland pony, black and white, 7 years old, good with kids - $50.00.

I was euphoric! It was the pony I had dreamed about. I read it again and showed it to Joel. "Yeah, that sounds like a good pony, but I don't know if Mom and Dad have $50.00. That's a lot of money."

I got a pencil and circled the advertisement. After supper, when Dad sat in the rocking chair to read the paper, I pointed it out to him. He read the ad out loud to Mother. "Dat's a lot uff money. Don't you sink, Katy?"

"Yes, but maybe we could trade something," Mom said. "The children sure would like a pony."

"All right. Da first rainy day when I can't work in da fields, I'll check it out."

"Yay! Yay!" we clamored. "Yippee, yippee, we're going to get a pony!"

The next few days dragged on. I kept hoping for rain, but sunny weather prevailed all week. One night I woke up to a familiar drumming sound on the roof. I jumped out of bed and opened the window.

"It's raining! It's raining!" I yelled to Joel, waking him up.

"So what?" He rubbed his bleary eyes, turned over and went back to sleep. I shut the window, and eventually fell asleep again.

About 5:30 A.M. as usual, our father came to the bottom of the stairs and called. "*Boova, boova, stehen auf!* (Boys, boys, get up!)" For once I bounced out of bed at the first call and ran to the window to check on the rain.

"It's still raining!" I called to Joel.

He wasn't impressed and took his time getting up. I yanked on my shirt and pants, ran to the stairway rail, straddled it , and zipped to the bottom. My appearance surprised Dad. He usually had to call at least twice to get us out from under those blankets.

"It's been raining all night," I said to Dad. "It sure would be a good day to go look at that pony."

"Ve vill see."

I could tell by the way he answered that I had better not press my luck. Instead, I worked like a busy beaver doing the chores and helping milk. I even offered to help him feed the hogs.

At the breakfast table Dad interrupted our chattering. He looked at Mom. "The boys and I are gonna go look at dat pony."

"Well, that's a good idea," Mother said. I was exuberant. My heart was racing, but I tried to portray calm.

After breakfast, Joel, Dad, and I got in the Model A and started driving toward Kokomo. As usual, Dad weaved back and forth along the Wildcat Creek Road as he looked at the neighbors' cornfields.

"Dis rain is sure gonna help da corn crop," he said.

Joel and I weren't interested in the corn; we were thinking about that pony. It seemed like Dad drove slower than ever. Finally he steered the car down a long lane to the pony owner's house and brought the Model A to a stop.

"Vell, boys, let's go see if the man still has dat pony."

As we walked toward the barn, the owner, a tall man in bib overalls and a green bill cap, came out of the house. He had a big paunch the overalls failed to hide.

"Good morning," he greeted us. "Can I help you?"

"Ve'd like to see da pony," Dad answered. "Dat's if you still haff it?"

"Yep, I do. It's sure a nice pony and would be just right for these boys." He placed a hand on each of our straw hats.

Beauty the Pony

We walked around the corner of the barn and there in a small pasture was the prettiest Shetland pony I had ever seen. Mostly black, it had white stocking feet, a big white patch across the shoulders that ran down each side, a white star on its forehead, and a neatly trimmed mane.

Joel and I looked at each other with awe. I could hardly contain my excitement, but Dad had warned us not to act too eager. "Maybe I can dicker with dis guy," he had told us on the way over.

The man talked and acted like a salesman. Dad tried to act nonchalant, but I saw the twinkle in his eye when he first saw the pony.

"How much do you vant for dis little mare?" Dad asked.

"Fifty dollars, it's a pure-bred Shetland pony."

"Dat's a lotta money," Dad said as he opened the pony's mouth and looked at its teeth.

"Seven years old," the man said.

"*Ya*. Dat's about right."

The owner looked at our eager faces.

"You can pet her. She's a gentle pony and just right for you boys."

Dad slowly lifted each leg, checked the pony's hooves carefully, and ran his hand over her hair, checking for blemishes. Physically the pony was perfect, and Dad was finding no faults he could dicker about. He hemmed and hawed, talked about the weather and how good the rain was for the corn crop and acted as if he wasn't too interested in the pony.

I could hardly contain myself. This was the perfect pony. I couldn't understand why Dad wasted time talking about the weather instead of just saying he would take it.

I blurted out. "Dad, what you going to do about the pony?"

He gave me a stern look but didn't answer my question. He and the man talked more about corn and hogs. Finally my father made an offer.

"I'll giff you forty dollars for dis pony."

The man shook his head. "No. It's worth every bit of fifty dollars.

Then they talked about corn and hogs again for twenty minutes while I fidgeted.

"Dad, what you gonna do about the pony?" I blurted out again. I just couldn't contain myself. I wanted that pony so bad, but I wasn't helping my father. Joel punched me in the ribs to shut me up.

"Joel, you take Willard and go sit in the car while dis man and I talk about the pony," Dad said.

I didn't want to go, but Joel grabbed my arm and we walked to the car. The two men stood and talked for another half-hour.

"Do you think we're going to get the pony?" I asked.

"Yes, if he can just dicker the man down a little."

"I don't see why it's taking so long."

It seemed like an eternity before I finally saw them shaking hands. I found out later that Dad had traded a sow, one runt pig and some cash to close the deal.

When Dad got back to the car, he gave me a stern lecture about bargaining and how you don't act too eager. Then he said, "I bought the pony!"

I was elated but thought I'd better hide my excitement or I would get another scolding.

That afternoon Dad hooked the four-wheeled trailer behind the Model A, then he and Joel drove back to get the pony. As punishment for spoiling his dickering, he didn't let me go along.

When Dad and Joel pulled up in front of the house with the pony, we all ran out, including our mother, who was holding Omar, our new baby brother. As Dad opened the gate and led the pony from the trailer, everyone oohed and aahed. "What a beautiful pony!" Mom said.

"Oh, she is a dandy!"

"What are we going to name her?" Almeda asked.

"Beauty," someone suggested, and we all agreed.

Dad got a bridle and harness in the trade but no saddle; our first riding would have to be bareback. "Who wants to ride first?" Mom asked.

"I do, I do, I do," came the cries.

"Little ones first," Mom said as she handed the baby to Almeda and helped little Miriam up on Beauty's back. Holding the bridle reins she led the pony in a big circle while Miriam clung onto the pony's mane. Then it was Sylvia's turn and then mine. I jumped on Beauty's back, grabbed the reins and said, "Giddyup." Beauty responded by walking ... very ... slowly. She was a gentle pony and used to kids, but could she run? I had always visualized myself galloping through the woods at full speed as the pony dodged around trees and leapt over logs. I yelled "Giddyup" again and slapped the leather reins on her shoulder. She broke into a stiff-legged trot. I bounced up and down like a jackhammer, barely staying on her back. The trot jarred my teeth until they clattered, but I couldn't get her to go any faster. I tried kicking her in the ribs, but since I was barefoot it had little effect.

Then came turns for Almeda and Joel. Beauty did the stiff-legged trot for them, too. The pony had us inexperienced kids figured out and was not going to give us a smooth ride. But I didn't give up. I had read how real cowboys used spurs on their boots to make horses run faster. I didn't have any spurs, but I did have a pair of hard leather shoes. I went in the house and got them. When I came out with my shoes on, I said, "Let me try again."

I leapt onto Beauty's back, shouted "Giddyup," gave her a slap with the reins, and kicked her in the ribs. She about jumped out from under me and immediately broke into a gallop. It was like riding a smooth rocking chair compared to that stiff-legged trot. We galloped down to the end of the lane, turned around, and galloped back.

"Boy, that Willard knows how to ride," Mom said.

"Wow! How did you do that?" Joel asked.

I was pretty proud of my performance and was soon giving the others advice on riding. Mom put Sylvia on the pony. "Now, Willard, you jump on behind Sylvia and show her how to ride." Again I kicked her in the ribs and we galloped down the lane as Sylvia hung on, laughing with delight.

A few weeks later Dad bought a small two-wheeled buggy at an auction for Beauty to pull. That fall a neighbor suggested that we boys use our pony and buggy to haul water for the local threshing ring. Joel and I anticipated getting rich. Dad, however, told us that if we were going to use Beauty on the hard gravel roads we would have to get her shod to protect her feet. We took her to a local blacksmith who charged two dollars for the shoeing job. That was a lot of money, immediately setting us back in our plan to become wealthy.

Joel and I worked together as water boys the first couple of days. Most of the farmers paid us ten cents for a half-day's job to haul water to the men in the fields. After the second day Joel decided we wouldn't get rich after all and told me I could do it. I think he feared we wouldn't make enough to pay for the shoeing job. I also was discouraged at making money, but I liked being a water boy. Dad saw my financial dilemma and said, "Since you use her to do a lotta work on the farm, I'll pay for da horse shoeing."

That statement surprised me, as Dad was pretty tight with his money, but it made me feel better since now all the dimes I took in were pure profit. The men in the fields liked seeing Beauty and me come around with the wooden keg of fresh, cold water. They kidded me and encouraged my work. After a bit of sage advice from a neighbor, I learned to deliver fresh water first to those who didn't chew tobacco. When I finished serving them, I again crossed the field and served the tobacco chewers. After I completed the round I drove to the water pump, rinsed the tobacco juice out of the keg, then filled it with clean cold water again. Everyone seemed happy with that arrangement, and I became a popular water boy. A few farmers gave me whole quarters for hauling water.

*Will Troyer at age 12 with Beauty the pony.
Omar is on the pony.*

One day, when I finished a job for a Mr. Miller, he said, "Now, Willard, you did a good job" and pressed a coin in my palm. I closed my hand on the coin and felt its large size. I bashfully said "Thank you" and drove off. When I got out of sight, I opened my fist and there lay a half-dollar! That was the biggest coin I had ever seen. I clutched it tightly all the way home. I unhitched Beauty, then ran to the house and showed it to my mother. "That's a lot of money, Willard," she said proudly. "Now put it in your piggy bank."

By the end of the threshing season I had earned three dollars, an unheard of sum for any of us kids. When I told my father how much I made, he said, "Willard, the pony belongs to all of you kids. You will have to share some of that money with the rest."

He suggested I keep half and divide the other half with my brothers and sisters. I was happy with that arrangement, as were my siblings.

All of us children rode and played with Beauty, but I spent nearly all my free time riding, grooming, and feeding her. We became inseparable. On Sunday afternoons I sometimes rode her over to the Deardorff farm. Ralph and his brother Roger also had a pony, as did their neighbor Bill Pearcy. We raced our ponies through the woods and pastures. I became a good rider and fancied myself a real cowboy, even though I didn't have a cowboy suit.

Eventually as I got older, I grew too big and heavy for Beauty. By then my smaller brothers, Phil and Omar, were old enough to ride. She was in our family for twenty years. One day after I left home, my mother wrote that they had sold Beauty. I was very disappointed. I thought that at age twenty-seven, Beauty had earned her retirement and should have been allowed to live out her life in the home pasture. I often wondered how long she lived and if she made some other children happy.

*Beauty hitched to a cart.
Will and Joel are standing; Miriam, Omar, and Sylvia are seated.*

14

DAD BUYS A TRACTOR

By the mid-1930s most farmers in Indiana used tractors, but a tractor had never been an option for my father while we were Amish. After we became Mennonites, only economics and personal preference dictated whether or not we would join the tractor revolution.

The 160-acre Smith farm was much larger than the McGrawsville place and required either more horses or a tractor. My father never made decisions hurriedly. He thought long and hard about the economics of using a tractor versus horses. He read many articles on the subject in his favorite farm magazine, the *Cappers Farmer*. The editors extolled the virtues of tractors in nearly every issue. He also argued the pros and cons of owning a tractor with many neighbors and friends.

One man could do a lot more work with a tractor than with horses. A farmer could start a tractor in the morning and be in the field plowing much quicker than he could harness a team of horses. He didn't need to rest the tractor when it got hot. It would run all day long. Nearly all tractors had power pulleys so they could be used on a belt to power various types of stationary machinery, such as a threshing machine or a hammer mill that ground corn and other grain for livestock feed. You didn't need to feed a tractor; it required fuel only while working. On the other hand, fuel could not be produced on a farm like horse feed, so it required a direct cash outlay, and there were no manure by-products to help enrich the soil.

The first spring we lived on the Smith farm, Dad hired Willard Sommers with his big Oliver tractor to do the spring plowing. Willard and his helper kept the Oliver going around the clock until the task was done. After that, we managed to do the soil preparation, spring planting, cultivating, haying, and crop harvesting with our five big draft horses and old Ben. We had sold Minor, the other buggy horse, when we bought the car.

One summer evening at the supper table in 1936, Dad announced, "Boys and girls, I haff some important news." We all stopped eating and looked up from our supper plates.

"Ve're gonna git a tractor." Mother smiled, as she had shared in this important decision. My sisters didn't have much to say, but Joel and I were electrified.

"A tractor!" Joel exclaimed. "What kind?"

"A John Deere Model A."

"New or used?" I didn't think my folks had enough money to buy a new one.

"Brand spanking new."

"Are you kidding us, Dad?"

"No, I'm not kiddin', it's a brand new tractor."

"Boy, oh boy!" Joel said. "A new tractor!"

"When we gettin' it?" I asked, still not convinced it was happening now.

"It vill be delivered in a few weeks."

Joel and I could hardly contain ourselves. All summer we had struggled and sweated driving horses in the field, while all around us we could hear the hum of our neighbors' tractors. George Ehrman had let us ride on his Farmall one day and had showed us how it worked. That hooked us boys on the merits of a tractor, although I still liked horses. "You don't even have to feed or harness a tractor," Joel argued. "Anyhow, if Dad buys one, we'll have to keep some horses to do a lot of the farm work."

He was right. My father would never sell all the horses. "I just hope he doesn't sell Bell," I said. She was gentle and my favorite horse.

About a month later we came home from school to find a brand new, bright green John Deere tractor in front of the barn. "Look!" Joel yelled, "the tractor!" and ran for the barn. I followed.

Just as we got to the tractor, Dad came out of the barn and watched us climb up on the seat. "Careful now, boys, it's no toy."

"Gee whiz, isn't this big!" I said "And I'll bet powerful! Boy, oh boy, what a machine!"

Tractors were almost indestructible in those days. Everything on that John Deere was made of iron and steel. Two huge rear steel wheels with long iron cleats provided plenty of traction when the weight of the heavy iron tractor sank into the soil. The rear axles rode high off the ground so they wouldn't knock over young grain crops. It had tricycle wheels, and the small front wheels placed together were centered between the large rear wheels, so you could straddle two cornrows and facilitate turns. The steering wheel and gas tank were also of steel as was the seat, although it had a steel spring which softened the jolts.

The tractor had a very short turning radius. By pushing one of the brakes and turning the front wheels sharply you could make it pivot around on the rear wheel. Thus it could make a sharp turn at the end of a field just like a team of horses.

Dad showed us how to start the tractor by turning on the gas, setting the choke and throttle, and opening the cockpits to reduce compression. Then he said, "Before you start it, make sure it's in neutral. Now stand back, boys."

He grabbed the big flywheel, which stuck out of the left side of the engine and gave it a forward spin. The John Deere immediately started firing and the familiar putt, putt sound of the two-cylinder engine drowned out our voices. Dad closed the cockpits, reduced the choke and throttle, and let the tractor idle.

"Now let me show ya how to drive it. Joel, you come first."

After he took Joel for a spin around the barn, he yelled at me, "Your turn, Willard."

I jumped up on the seat beside him. He showed me how to engage the gears by pushing in the hand clutch. Then he let me drive around the barn lot, work the gas lever and the clutch. Joel and I were elated that we got to drive the tractor.

"Now, let's see if you boys can start it." By that he wanted to know if we could turn the big flywheel. Joel managed to turn it over; then I stood in front of the rear wheel, grabbed the flywheel with both hands, and pulled, but I just couldn't turn it. I grunted and pulled several times without success. "Dat's all right, Willard, I can start it for you till you git bigger."

I was relieved, because I was afraid he wouldn't let me drive until I could start it.

He warned us not to drive it in fourth gear, its top speed. With the throttle wide open it would go about 6½ mph, the iron cleats tossing dirt high, sending an occasional clod of dirt onto the back of the driver. But it didn't take us long to open it up when Dad wasn't around.

After the quick lesson with the tractor, Joel and I went to the barn to do the evening chores. Two of our draft horses were missing, traded in on the tractor. He had dickered with the dealer getting quite a bit off the $600 price of the tractor for a team of horses. He did this trading while we were in school and was probably happy I wasn't around to spoil his dickering again.

I ran to the horse stalls to see if Bell, my favorite, was still around. I found three draft horses, Bell, Corey, and Doll, and Ben, the ex-buggy horse. I was relieved.

We used the horses to pull wagons while making hay, threshing, shucking corn, and hauling manure. Horses were also used to plant corn, mow hay, and perform a lot of other tasks, so they were still essential on our farm after we got the tractor.

Most of our immediate neighbors had Farmall, Allis-Chalmers, or Oliver tractors. We were the only ones with a John Deere and because of its distinctive putt, putt, we came in for a lot of ribbing. As soon as George Ehrman heard the John Deere, he drove over. "What's that funny popping noise disturbing the neighborhood?" he joked.

The next morning Lee Miller, one of our neighbors, approached Joel and me while we waited for the school bus. "Your dad buy a tractor?"

"Yep, it's a brand new John Deere."

"Yeah, I can tell that." He smiled and spat a big stream of tobacco juice onto a fence post. "That's all I wanna know," he said and headed back to his house. Lee was a good neighbor but never one to waste words.

That spring, Dad purchased a two-bottom tractor plow the John Deere could pull in second gear. It was expensive to buy new equipment for the tractor. Dad converted some of our old horse implements over so they could be pulled with the John Deere. He welded a tractor hitch onto our horse-drawn disk, then he chained the spike-toothed harrow behind it. The John Deere was capable of pulling both implements. It had taken four horses to pull the disk and another team to drag the harrow.

He also put a tractor hitch on the two-row horse cultivator, but two years later he bought a mounted tractor cultivator that eliminated the need for two people to cultivate corn.

I was ten years old when we got the John Deere and gradually learned how to operate it with all the different equipment. By the time I was twelve, I was capable of doing about every farm task.

I often got bored sitting on the machine, plowing or cultivating for ten or twelve hours a day. I passed the time by singing loudly, knowing the putt, putt of the tractor would drown out any failings I had as singer. I would go through all the hymns I learned at church and some versions I didn't learn there. I sang "At the bar, at the bar where I smoked my first cigar," with gusto, knowing my mother was unable to hear this sacrilegious variant of the hymn "At the Cross." I also sang popular songs of the day, such as "Home on the Range" and "Deep in the Heart of Texas." These were wanderlust songs, for I continued to dream of living out west with the cowboys. I thought it would be a much more romantic life than driving a tractor around and around the fields for hours at a time. I planned my future on that tractor and yearned to go to all the far places of the world. Of course my parents wanted all of us kids to be farmers as their ancestors had been, so I kept my fantasies to myself.

Dad was slow in adopting new farming devices, which frustrated me as I got older. Soon after we got the tractor, most farmers were converting theirs to rubber tires. The steel wheels on our John Deere slipped and spun in loose, plowed soil while the big rubber tires on our neighbor's tractors packed down the soil, as they pulled without slipping. I tried to talk my dad into getting rubber tires, but he continued to doubt their merits. Eventually Dad was convinced and bought rubber-tired wheels.

The durable John Deere remained in the family for many years. It was almost indestructible and was repaired or overhauled many times when some part quit functioning. My two younger brothers Omar and Philip also grew up driving the John Deere. Dad finally sold it, still in good working condition, when he retired from farming in the mid-1960s. I suspect that if I could find it in some farmer's implement graveyard today, put gas in the tank, set the choke and the gas lever, and spin the big flywheel, the old John Deere would rise from its long silence with a *putt, putt, putt*.

15

THE BLIZZARD OF '36

The first early morning snowflakes fell softly on the lawn and windowsills, shattering silently into tiny pieces. Soon more tumbled from the sky, clothing the lawn with a white blanket. By the time we had done the morning chores, eaten breakfast, and were ready for school, several inches of snow covered the ground and clung to fence posts and tree branches, hiding the drab late fall colors that had dominated the landscape.

We trudged through the snow to the end of the lane to catch the school bus. As we waited, a light north wind began to swirl the snow, piling it against the sides of fences, trees, and roadsides. By the time the driver had picked up the last kids, the weather had turned into a blinding snowstorm. The driver could barely see the road, but he knew the route like the back of his hand, and we arrived at school right on schedule, as did all the other buses.

At recess time some of us went outside to play, but driven by the strong wind, the pelting snow stung our faces, so we retreated inside.

In music class, just before the noon break, Miss Stout kept glancing out the window as she led us through various musical exercises.

"Looks like a real blizzard out there," she said.

Miss Stout lived in New London and had some winding, hilly roads to travel on her way home.

We were in our homeroom eating lunch when the principal walked in. "The superintendent just called. We're going to send you home early."

Several students cheered. Mrs. Smith clapped her hands to quiet us. "The bus drivers are on the way," the principal continued, "and as soon as they get here, you'll leave."

When the buses came, we streamed out the door into the storm. We struggled for a few minutes to find our buses but were soon loaded and headed home. Snowdrifts had already formed on the roads, and the bus lurched whenever it hit one. Several miles from the school, a big drift jolted the bus to a sudden stop. The driver tried to back out, but the wheels just spun. Then he asked all of us boys to get off and push.

The cold gusty wind stung our faces as we waded through the deep snow to the front of the bus. When the driver revved the engine, someone yelled, "O.K., let's push!"

We heaved against the front bumper and fender with all our might. The spinning rear wheels sent snow flying, but the bus failed to move. Suddenly it broke free and the bus driver backed into a driveway a hundred feet back before letting us in. Snow clung to our clothes as we stomped onto the bus and sat down.

"Now kids, we're not gonna make it home. Wildcat Creek Road will be a lot worse than this one. I'm going to take you back to school. Doncha worry, you'll be O.K."

At first there was silence, then someone piped up, "Maybe we'll get to spend the night at school!"

"Yeah, won't that be fun!"

After bucking through a few more snowdrifts, our driver got us back to school. The teachers were gone, but the janitor was still there. We ran downstairs to the gym. In a few minutes the bus driver and janitor called us together. "We have to spend the night here. Doncha worry, the place is warm; there's some food in the Home Ec room and there are blankets."

"What'll our folks think when we don't come home?" someone asked.

"We're gonna phone all your parents."

While we were standing around excitedly contemplating our stay, the gym door opened. Miss Stout and another teacher walked in. They had also been unable to get home.

We didn't have a phone at home and I wondered if Dad and Mom would worry about us. I asked Almeda what she thought. "I told Miss Stout to call the Lee Millers. I'm sure he'll walk over and tell Mom and Dad."

The older kids, the teachers, and the janitor started looking around for bedding and found enough blankets stored in various rooms. There were plenty of wrestling and tumbling mats in the gym to serve as mattresses.

Someone called Ed Lovelace, who lived about a mile from school. The Lovelace family got together some blankets and food, including a great big ham, piled everything on their big Farmall tractor, and Mr. Lovelace drove it through the big drifts to school. Now we were in good shape. "If you need anything else, let me know!" he yelled as he climbed back on the tractor and disappeared into the whiteout.

During the afternoon we entertained ourselves by playing games such as basketball and tag. A couple of us boys decided to go outside for a few minutes, but the blizzard blasted our bare faces and we retreated inside for the rest of the day. By evening the adults had managed to cook up the ham, along with some other food they found in the Home Ec room. We had plenty to eat. Then one of the older boys got a bright idea. "Why don't we break into the candy room?"

"Sure, we can have candy for dessert," another agreed.

Each year the senior class sold candy from a small room in the building to raise money for their graduation. Miss Stout agreed to the plan, considering the circumstances, and in a few minutes some of the bigger boys had removed the hinges from the candy room door. It felt like Christmas again as we were each given a small supply of candy.

We spent the rest of the evening playing and reading. About 10 P.M. the adults announced it was time to go to bed. We dragged the mats and blankets onto the gym floor and started to settle down. The giggling and whispering continued for some time, but gradually the place became silent.

The next morning we were up early. A peek outside revealed that the blizzard had stopped, leaving behind a calm white winter wonderland. The snowplow crews had begun clearing the roads long before daylight, but since it would take some time to open all the rural roads, the superintendent canceled school for another day. By 11 A.M. our bus driver announced we would be leaving. A few of us groaned, hoping to spend another night.

Mom met us at the door when we got home. "Now, stomp off your boots outside. So, you kids got stuck in school."

"How did you find out?" I wanted to know.

"Lee Miller walked over and told us. Didja have plenty to eat?"

We told her about all the playing we got to do, and how we broke into the candy room. "You kids were lucky. I was afraid you might get stuck in the middle of the road."

A few days later there was a sudden change in the weather. The thermometer climbed into the 40s and the snow began to melt. Then a freezing rain fell on Saturday night. By Sunday morning the snow was gone; icicles hung from the eaves. Everything was encased in ice. The twigs and small branches in the tree tops tinkled in the breeze. Some branches broke from the weight of the ice and came crashing down. The ground was covered with an inch-and-a-half of ice. We half slid, half walked on our way to the barn to feed the livestock and milk the cows.

"Mom, don't you think it's too icy to drive to church?" I asked hopefully after breakfast.

"No. We will just drive slowly. Now hurry up and get dressed."

We piled into the Model A and Mother drove cautiously down the lane. It was slick, and when she tried to stop at the gate, the car slid ten feet. This should have deterred my parents from continuing the fifteen miles to church, but they were determined. Missing church was never considered, except in case of severe sickness.

Mother drove about 20 mph. We had gone five miles when the front wheel caught a rut in the road, and the car started to spin. Mother screamed and spun the wheel. In a split second the Model A had turned 180 degrees and come to a stop on the edge of the road. Dad looked down into the eight-foot deep ditch. "Katy, it's zu icy. *Vella heim gehen* (Let's go home.)"

After we heard our father's comment, everyone was silent for a moment. I elbowed Joel in the ribs. "Maybe we can go sledding," I whispered.

As soon as we got home, Joel and I shed our Sunday clothes, grabbed the sled, and headed for the top of the lane. Joel lay flat on the sled and I lay on top of him. We pushed off and gained speed as we glided down the icy surface toward the bridge, then zipped up the hill to the end of the lane. We were going too fast to stop at the gate, and I was sure we were going to crash, but Joel turned the runners hard, stuck out his foot and spun the sled. It hit a rock and rolled us over.

"Boy, that was fun! Let's do it again!" Joel said, laughing.

We zoomed down the lane repeatedly, crashing numerous times, then Joel got the bright idea to go ice-skating. We went to the house to get our skates. Mom saw us. "Now boys, dinner is about ready. You wait till after dinner before you go again. The girls also want to go, so you have to share the sled with them."

"They can have the sled. We're going ice-skating," I said.

Everyone was eager to play. Miriam and Sylvia decided to go sledding while Almeda opted to skate with us. We clamped the skates onto the soles of our leather shoes and headed outside.

None of us were good skaters. We wobbled cautiously around in circles. Finally I glided down the lane and the others followed, but before I got to the bridge, I was out of control and fell. Almeda and Joel crashed into me. We whooped and hollered, got onto our feet and continued. The ice-encrusted lane had some rough spots and we landed on our rear ends numerous times. At the end of the lane Joel said, "I'll bet we could skate on the road. Let's try it!"

Almeda and I were game and soon the three of us were gliding past the Miller house. The road was one long ice rink. We skated by the Ehrmans and the Claude Wikel place before turning around and heading back. George Ehrman saw us and came out to see what we were up to.

"Wow, that looks like fun," he said. "I'll get Eva and the kids."

Near our lane we saw a lone skater coming from the other direction. It turned out to be Donald Smith, our neighbor's son who tapped our maple trees. After an hour or two, our feet were tired and we headed home. We told Mother how we had skated on the icy road. "It's hard to believe," she said. "I don't think this has happened before. I just can't remember so much snow and ice in one week. You kids will remember this the rest of your lives."

16

LIVESTOCK AND PETS

Many animals lived on our farm, but only one became a hero, our collie Trixie. The family was in the orchard picking apples when Sylvia, who was five years old, wandered off toward the barn. Without realizing it, she got close to a large white sow with a new litter of pigs. When Sylvia saw the sow, she got scared, screamed, and ran. The protective sow apparently mistook her high-pitched scream for a pig squeal and thought Sylvia had caught one of her offspring. She took after Sylvia, who was running as fast as her little legs could carry her. All of us heard her scream and watched, momentarily frozen in horror, as the sow gave chase. Dad started running, but he would never get there in time. That's when Trixie shot past Dad toward the sow. "Git 'er, Trixie! Git 'er!" Dad yelled, but he didn't need to.

In seconds Trixie slammed into the sow and grabbed her by an ear. The sow started squealing with pain and fighting to break the dog's hold, but Trixie held on even though she was slammed to the ground several times. Dad continued running and yelling for Trixie to hang on. Sylvia was still screaming but rapidly gaining ground from the sow.

The chaotic episode lasted less than two minutes. With her arms wrapped around Mother's neck, Sylvia was crying from fright as Mom tried to comfort her. Trixie kept her teeth clenched on the sow's ear until Dad commanded the dog to let go. Once released, the sow, dripping blood from a badly torn ear, ran back to her piglets. We all knew our dog had saved Sylvia's life and thereafter Trixie was elevated to the status of a hero in our family.

All the livestock and pets on our farm had a purpose. The dairy cows produced milk that was the major source of our farm income; their calves were butchered for meat and also sold on the livestock market for cash. The horses were used to work the fields and pull buggies or wagons. We had about a hundred laying hens that produced eggs for the table, the surplus eggs being sold on the market. Another hundred to two hundred young chickens were raised each year for meat and the remainder sold for cash. The hundred or so young pigs we fed our corn to and marketed each fall were the second major source of income on our farm. We also had about twenty sheep that brought in a modest amount of cash twice a year. The adults were sheared each spring and the wool sold. We fattened the young lambs through the summer and sold them on the market in the fall. Dad valued them most highly because they ate weeds that other livestock shunned.

In addition to protecting small children and serving as watchdogs and pets, our farm dogs helped herd cows, horses, and sheep. Our ubiquitous cats—we had up to seventeen at times—caught mice and rats. Since rodents could destroy lots of grain, Dad considered the cats of major economic importance, but my sisters loved them just as pets.

To save time we trained the livestock to come when called. A loud booming "*Whoop! Whoop! Whoop! Whoop Ben!*" brought in the horses. Cows answered to "*Sooook! Soook! Sook! Sook! Sook!*" and the hogs came to a shriller "*Zooooiee! Zooooieee!*" Usually the animals came in anticipation of being fed, but if they weren't hungry, they often stayed put. If they didn't respond, I jumped on Beauty the pony's back and raced to the fields or woods to bring them in.

Other farmers also called livestock and we could often hear the long thundering calls of a nearby farmer reverberate across the rural landscape in the stillness of a morning or evening. All farmers' calls were distinctive, and we always knew which neighbor was attempting to bring in his livestock.

In addition to cats and dogs, we often had livestock for pets. Whenever a dairy cow gave birth to a calf, it was weaned as soon as possible to get the mother back to producing milk for us. We kids had the task of teaching the calf to drink milk from a pail, which was not natural to the calves.

Joel and I always worked together to train a calf, one of us holding the animal by the neck while the other stuck a finger in its mouth to simulate its mother's teat. Once the calf began sucking on my finger, I lowered my hand and the calf's head into a bucket of milk. After a few lessons the calf drank from the pail on its own. In the process we became the calves' surrogate mothers, and they followed us around the farm like pets.

One of our pet calves was Ginger. When she got larger, Joel suggested, "Let's make her a riding calf. She should be just as much fun to ride as Beauty."

I said, "Oh, I don't know, Joel. Most calves don't like to be ridden."

But Joel was persuasive and soon we had a halter on Ginger and a tight leather strap cinched just behind her shoulder. The calf was very docile and didn't attempt to fight the strap, which put me at ease. "Now, Willard, you wanna be a cowboy, so here's your chance to practice."

Joel helped me get on Ginger's back. I'd expected her to run immediately, but she stood still. I kicked her in the ribs like I did the pony, but she wouldn't move. "This calf's not gonna run," I told Joel.

"Just a minute. I'll twist her tail a bit."

He grabbed her tail, formed it into a big circle, and then gave it a snap. The calf leapt in the air and started bucking. Joel yelled, "Hold on!" That was unnecessary advice as I was hanging onto the strap with both hands. On the first jump my big straw hat went sailing through the air and on about the third jump I did the same. I landed on my shoulder right into a fresh cow paddy and slid through two or three more before I came to a stop. When I stood up I had cow manure all over my shirt, pants, and face.

Joel roared with laughter. "Ya look like a real cowboy, Willard! Ha, ha, ha!"

I glared at him, reached for a cow paddy to throw as he took off running and laughing. Mom was in the yard and heard all the commotion and came to investigate. She took one look at my decorated clothes and face.

"What in the world are you two up to!" she yelled. "Now, doncha even think of goin' into the house with that mess!"

"It was Joel's fault," I mumbled.

"I don't care whose fault it was, you get over there by the pump and get those clothes off, Willard!" Then she joined Joel in laughter before ordering him to go into the house and get me clean clothes.

We rarely had pigs for pets and I didn't hold them in high esteem. They wallowed in mud holes, rooted through cow manure to eat undigested corn kernels, fought, squealed and, because of their dirty habits, stunk! But we liked to eat pork, and Dad depended on hog sales for cash income.

I hated ringing pigs. We accomplished the job by putting split copper rings into their tender snouts to discourage them from rooting up soil in the fields and pastures. Joel and I took turns catching a small pig, grabbing it by both ears, and holding the struggling animal between our legs in a sitting position while Dad, using a pliers, pinched a ring in the pig's nose. The pigs would squeal constantly, making it almost impossible to hear Dad's directives. Our pants, boots, and hands got filthy dirty and Mother forbade us to enter the house after ringing pigs until we had washed and changed pants.

Placing rings into the snout of a mature sow or boar was worse. Dad made a hog catcher for this operation. The device consisted of a steel pipe about four or five feet long, through which was threaded a heavy wire. The pipe was attached to a rod that slid inside it. The rod could be thrust down to form a loop in the wire at the bottom. While the hog was confined to a small pen, Dad slipped the loop into the hog's mouth and over its nose, then yanked on the pipe handle to cinch the loop. He wrestled the hog to a standstill as it fought to break free, squealing at the top of its lungs! As a young boy I often sat on the sidelines with my eyes shut and fingers in my ears until Dad had the hog subdued. Then Joel and I worked together to hold the struggling pig while Dad pinched four or five rings in the hog's nose. After the rings were installed, the wire loop on the hog catcher was opened and the hog released. Boars would sometimes turn and try to attack us when they were released, so we were always ready to jump over the fence.

Young male pigs raised for meat production also had to be castrated. I hated this job worse than hog ringing, but castrated pigs would gain weight rapidly and produce quality meat.

We first separated the pigs from their mothers, then confined them to a small pen. I would catch a pig by a hind leg and drag it out of the pen fighting and squealing to where Dad was waiting. I flipped the pig on its side, then held a front and rear foot together with both hands while kneeling on its neck to subdue it. Dad slit the scrotum with a sharp knife and removed the testicles. He then poured an ample supply of disinfectant into the bleeding cavity. I then released the pig and let it run outside where the sow was waiting.

I didn't like the job of castrating pigs, and in retrospect it seems cruel, but it was one of those tasks on the farm that was necessary. I'm sure they use more humane methods today.

*Miriam, Joel, Sylvia, and little Omar
with a pet lamb at the Smith farm*

Our most common livestock pets were lambs. Every spring we kids had the task of feeding one or more orphaned lambs. Ewes were gentle and usually good mothers, but occasionally a ewe would reject her lamb, refusing to let it suckle. Dad would catch the ewe, forcing her to let the lamb feed. After a few tries the ewe often accepted the lamb. If she continued to reject her offspring, we hand-fed it. At times ewes didn't have enough milk for their lambs, so we got to bottle feed those, too. Either way was good news for us kids. We loved pet lambs. They were gentle and quickly adopted us as parents, following us almost everywhere.

Dad sometimes let us keep young animals as our own to raise and sell. The money we earned from the lambs was in lieu of an allowance. As we got older, we were given more opportunities to make money from livestock and pets. For several summers in my teens I was given fifty chicks to raise and sell. It was my duty to feed them and eventually butcher the young fryers for the market. Sometimes I raised a calf or a pig. I always took special care of my personal animals and chickens. These projects taught me how to care for the livestock and gave me an even greater sense of being part of the family farm operation.

I raised some mallard ducks one year. Mom got fifteen eggs from a neighbor, and I set them under a brooding hen. Soon after the eggs hatched, the fluffy ducklings jumped into a puddle of water. This drove the hen crazy, because chickens don't swim. She clucked and attempted to call them away from the puddle, but they kept on swimming. She waded into the shallow edge of the water and they swam to her, but as she headed for shore they again bolted for the deep water. Once through swimming, the ducklings followed the hen to dry land, but whenever she got near any water, they again caught the urge to swim. It drove the poor mother hen batty; she must have wondered what was wrong with her crazy chicks.

While rearing the mallards, I decided to try something I had read about in a book. A guy had banded some of his tame mallard ducks and let them go south in the fall. The next spring they returned bringing a bunch of other ducks with them. I thought this sounded like a good way to get into the duck business, so I banded six of my mallards and didn't clip their wings. Toward fall the young ducks began flying around, and one day I watched them join a flock of wild ducks and fly south. I had the urge to follow, and all winter I dreamed of getting a whole bunch of ducks back. In the spring I scanned the skies and hoped my six mallards would lead a big flock to the barnyard, but like myself when I eventually left the farm, they never returned.

17

ELECTRICITY COMES TO OUR HOUSE

The Amish church doesn't allow the use of electricity, but the Mennonites do. When we became Mennonites, however, this modern convenience was still not available in our rural neighborhood. We didn't miss it, though, since we had never experienced its usefulness. We used several other methods to produce light and power.

My parents had a number of single-globe kerosene lamps, which we referred to as coal oil lights. Wicks sucked kerosene from the bottom of the lamp. When you needed a light you removed the globe, turned up the wick, lit it with a match, and then adjusted the flame before replacing the globe. These lamps were rather dim by today's standards but were a considerable improvement over a candle. Even so, you had to sit fairly close to the kerosene lamp to have enough light to read. We had several in the house and carried them from room to room as we needed them.

We often had two lamps in the living room after supper, but with five or six of the family wanting to read or play, it was not unusual for three or four of us kids to crowd around one dim kerosene lamp.

"Mom, Willard's hoardin' all the light," one of my sisters would often complain.

"Now, Willard, you scoot over and let the others share the light," Mom would say.

I would grudgingly move to a dimmer spot while others crowded in closer. If one of us needed to go to another room, we carried a lamp with us. That often started a fight between us kids, and the dispute had to be settled by our parents.

We also had a kerosene-fueled light called an Aladdin lamp. It had a tall glass globe and a mantle. It produced about twice the light of a regular kerosene lamp. We used the Aladdin lamp only when we had company or for special occasions. Aladdin lamps used more fuel and the lamps and mantles were more expensive to buy and maintain than the kerosene wick lamps.

For working in the barn or outdoors at night we used lanterns. These were similar to the house lamps but much sturdier. Each had a steel top with holes to release the heat, a wire handle for carrying, and a steel frame around the glass globe for protection. Dad would light the lantern after supper, then head to the barn to check on the livestock. I often peered out the window and watched the lantern light cast long shadows of my dad walking.

In the winter when darkness came early, chores were done by lantern light. We usually hung two on the walls behind the cows and milked by the dim glow. If we needed to go to the haymow or to the horse shed we carried a lantern. During the long winter nights Dad hung one in the chicken house to encourage the hens to lay more eggs.

We also used kerosene to help raise chickens. We hatched the chicks each spring in a kerosene egg brooder, which kept the eggs at the same constant temperature as a hen sitting on a clutch of eggs. We turned the eggs once or twice a day to simulate the actions of a brooding hen. I sure got excited to hear the first peep, peep of the newly emerging chicks. I loved to help remove the small fluffy chicks from the brooder and place them in the warm brooder house that was heated with kerosene as well.

Kerosene was also a fuel source for cooking meals. Mother did most of her cooking on a four-burner kerosene stove in the summer, to avoid excessive heat in the house. In the winter, however, she used the big wood-burning kitchen range, which also helped to keep the kitchen warm. Our central heating system was a pot-bellied stove that sat in the living room and burned wood or coal. It was our only other source of heat in the winter. On cold nights everyone crowded around the stoves to keep warm.

We had neither a refrigerator nor a freezer. Mother canned most of our meat, fruit, and vegetables. She kept leftovers, milk, butter, and other fresh food for a few days in a cool room. Usually this room was in the pump house above the deep well, as the temperature of the well water far below the ground surface always remained cool. Some of our neighbors had iceboxes, the forerunner of the modern refrigerator.

Large blocks of ice were put in the bottom of the cooler; in warm weather you had to replace the ice every few days. The ice could be purchased from neighbor Hugh Smith for a few cents a block. He cut the ice from his pond every winter, stashed it in a shed, and layered it with sawdust. The ice, which kept all summer, was another source of income for Mr. Smith.

Like most farmers we hand-pumped water from our well. Some wells had windmills that kept the big livestock water tanks full, but ours didn't. Our only source of artificial power was a small 1½ horse, one-cylinder gas engine with a pulley. We used it to run the small grinding mills, corn shellers, and other mechanical devices. While it saved us labor, it sometimes created work, too. To get it started, you had to spin the heavy steel flywheel with a hand crank. At times it refused to start after numerous attempts, and Dad would kick it in frustration. Eventually, after he tinkered with the gas adjustment and choke, the little engine would start to putt, putt.

Doing the wash in the early days was strictly a hand-powered job, but as our family grew, my mother had more and more piles of clothes to wash every Monday morning. It was a burden to wash by hand so Dad installed a pulley on the washer, cut a hole in the wall of the pump house, and ran a belt outside to the gas engine. This saved Mother a lot of time and energy but not without some cost. When Dad wasn't nearby, Mom would try to start the engine herself. Whenever the engine failed to start, she would shout at it in frustration. "Now, why don'cha start? Ya dirty aggravatin' machine!"

After four or five such attempts she lost hope. "Willard, go to the barn and git yer dad," she'd say, throwing the crank on the ground in defeat. "If we ever, *ever* get electricity, the first thing I'm gonna do is git an electric washer."

Many farms in central Indiana had electricity by the time we moved to the Smith farm in 1935, but ours was not one of them. Then in early 1937 the local electric company announced it would have power in our neighborhood by fall. Since my parents had never lived where electricity was available, they had a lot of planning to do. The house was brick, so the wiring had to be installed on the surface of the walls. Mom and Dad debated the placement of lights in each room, how many there should be and the number and wattage of the bulbs. Dad figured the barn required lots of light and installed 100-watt bulbs in the haymow, the milking parlor, and the horse shed.

In a few weeks we got the house and barn wired and the bulbs installed. We turned on all the switches so we would know when the electricity arrived. We were now anxious to have electricity, and for weeks our conversation around the dinner table was dominated about how nice it would be when the "artificial lights" came on. Another month went by and we began to doubt we would actually get electricity. Perhaps it was only a dream. Then one evening, we were dazzled with bright lights. It was a stunning experience. We whooped, hollered, and danced in celebration. "Yay, we got electricity! Whoopee! Whoopee! We got electricity!"

Then we ran around the house to check every room to see if the lights were working. We were practically blinded by this sudden display of intense illumination. I stood in one room and flipped the same switch off and on at least a dozen times, not quite believing that it really worked. I ran outside and saw that Lee Miller, our nearest neighbor, also had lights. Dashing back inside, I yelled to the rest of the family, "Come out. I can see Lee Miller's lights!"

The whole family came running into the yard to look at the Miller's lights. We couldn't see George Ehrman's house, but we heard his family celebrating a half-mile away. Then Hugh Smith rang his big brass bell in joyful celebration.

It was a big moment in our rural neighborhood, and electricity would gradually change our lives. We no longer needed to light kerosene lamps or carry them around the house; with the flick of a switch we had lights in every room. We could now sit any place in the living room and read. A yard light between the house and the barn eliminated the need for carrying a lantern between buildings. It was almost like having constant daylight.

We boys were especially overwhelmed with the lights in the barn. You could see everywhere. Dad thought it was almost too bright, and when the first electric bill came he started reducing the size of the bulbs throughout the barn.

Electricity was a real revolution for our family, but it was a long time before we acquired any major electrical gadgets, except for one. Mother had vowed to get an electric washing machine, and Dad knew that it was one thing that would make her extremely happy. About a week before we got electricity, Dad announced at the supper table, "Your mom and I are goin' to Kokomo in da morning to look for an electric washin' machine."

Mother beamed with delight. "Just think, before long I won't hafta crank that old engine. Washin' will be a delight."

They left early the next morning and when they returned, they had a brand new Speed Queen washer. They put it in the pump house next to the old washer and there it sat until the night we got electricity.

While the rest of us were still dazzled and experimenting with the bright lights, Mom went to the pump-house to plug in her new washer. The motor hummed as she ran the washer through all its paces. She then called to the rest of us, "Come see my new washer!"

We kids stood around in amazement as she demonstrated the new machine. Even the wringers were turned by electricity - no more hand cranking! Then she announced. "I'm gonna wash right now," and walked to the bedroom for a hamper full of dirty clothes. Meanwhile, we had gone back to trying out the new lights. Then we heard Mom singing in the pump house in her loud soprano voice…"Rock of ages, cleft for me…."

Dad looked up from reading the paper and grinned at us kids. "I sink your Mom's happy with dat washer."

18

OLD BEN

The two large scars Old Ben had on each buttock portrayed the horse's character. He was rebellious and defiant, often getting into fights with his teammates when he was in the barn lot. But to us, his most definitive characteristic was his mischievous habit of always watching for an opportunity to run away while hitched to a wagon or buggy.

A lightweight, sorrel-colored horse, Ben stood over sixteen hands high and had a broad white stripe down his forehead. Dad acquired him from a neighbor, Joel Graber, soon after I was born. He used him as a dual-purpose horse, hitching him to a buggy on Sundays and working him in the field during the week.

Old Ben caused my family and me considerable trauma in the years we had him. My first dramatic experience occurred when I was five years old. My sister Sylvia and I accompanied Mother on an errand to our cousin's house. On our return, Mother saw our neighbor, Ale Kate, working in her garden near the road and stopped to talk. She got out of the buggy to visit. After about fifteen minutes Mother returned to the buggy, but just before she climbed aboard, she thought of another piece of juicy gossip to share with her neighbor. Leaning beside the buggy she stretched the story out for another five minutes. By this time Old Ben, hitched to the buggy with Minor, was getting antsy. He turned his head several times to look at Mother, then bobbed his head up and down and slobbered as if to say, "Get aboard and let's go home."

Mother, forgetting Old Ben's outlaw ways, ignored this gesture and continued to chat. Suddenly Ben snorted and started prancing forward. Mother grabbed onto the buggy with both hands and yelled, "Whoa, Ben! Whoa!" Ben seemed to sense her precarious position and started to run, dragging Mother, who was in danger of being run over by the rear wheel. While Ale Kate lifted her long Amish skirt and started running, to intercept the horses, Mother continued yelling, "Whoa!" but Ben just ran faster, encouraging Minor along. Still sitting in the buggy, my sister and I were nearly frozen with fear, but then my training took over. I already knew how to drive horses. I grabbed the driving lines with my little hands and jerked on the right line as hard as I could. The horses responded, turned to the right and came to a quick halt when the buggy shaft caught in the roadside fence. Mother jumped up into the buggy, grabbed the lines, and jerked the bit in Old Ben's mouth repeatedly, forcing Ben's head up and down like a yo-yo.

"Now, you little monster, you know better than try and run off with me!" she screamed.

After yelling at the horse she praised me, "Willard, you did real good turnin' those mean horses. You're gonna be a real horseman when you grow up."

I was still shaking from the episode, but I was so proud of Mother's praise that my buttons almost popped off my shirt.

When we got home, Mother told my father about mean Old Ben and related our narrow escape.

"Ja, I guess I'm gonna hafta git rid of dat horse," he said, but he didn't.

Old Ben often worked gently and diligently all day in the field with other horses, then toward the end of the day, when he thought it was time to quit, he practically sprinted around the field. When he was in a going-home mood, you had to keep your eye on him constantly as he always waited for an opportunity to bolt for home.

One time I had Ben and Cory hitched to a wagon, loading hay. I had just about finished the high load and was at the back of the wagon leveling the hay with a pitchfork and out of sight of the horses. Apparently Ben looked back at that moment and, unable to see me, sensed an opportunity to run for home. The team jumped forward in their traces, nearly knocking me off the load, then galloped through the field. I regained my feet and managed to get to the front of the bouncing wagon and grab the lines. I yelled "Whoa!" and pulled on the lines, but Old Ben had taken the bridle bit in his teeth and clenched down. Pull as I might, I couldn't stop that team. We flew through the hay field and into the apple orchard, where a big apple tree knocked off my big straw hat and nearly scraped me off the load. Past the orchard, the run-away team sent a flock of chickens flying and squawking, trampling two to death. We then barreled into the barnyard, scattering cows and hogs in every direction. Near the barn Ben made a sudden turn, flipping the load of hay and me to the ground. Luckily the soft hay broke my fall so I wasn't hurt. The horses ran another two hundred feet farther, then stopped with their heads against the barn door, winded and panting but unrepentant.

Another day Dad, Joel, and I were shucking a load of corn. All three of us briefly got toward the rear of the wagon. Old Ben had been turning his head and watching, then sensed an opportunity. He jumped forward in his traces, enticing the other horse in the team to run also. Dad sprinted for the wagon, but it was too late. The team galloped through the cornfield. The wagon bounced over some ruts and the tailgate came off, scattering ears of corn across the field. They raced through a small pasture and to the barn before they stopped. When Dad caught up, he yanked the lines and yelled, "I'll teach ya to run away, ya ol' rascal." He then took the loose ends of the leather lines and whacked Old Ben across the rump until he quivered with fright, but this still didn't deter the outlaw horse.

Old Ben's rebelliousness included never letting anyone ride him. A few had tried, but they always ended up on the ground. I forgot about that one day when Dad put me in the field to cultivate corn with Old Ben and another horse. I was only ten years old. About mid-morning one of the lines caught on the hames of Ben's harness. To untangle the lines, I walked out on the steel tongue between the horses and leaned over on Ben's back. Apparently afraid I was going to climb on his back, he bolted and, leading the other horse, they raced across the cornfield at a full gallop. From my precarious position on the steel tongue I couldn't stop them, so I leaned over, grabbed the other horse's hames and hung on for dear life. The cultivator shovels, still in the ground, tore through the corn plants, sending the large green stalks flying ten to twelve feet into the air and raising a cloud of dust. Dad and Joel, who were working on the other side of the field with the tractor and another cultivator, saw the runaway team and came running toward the galloping horses. When the team came to the fence at the end of the field, they stopped and I jumped off. I was shaking like a leaf when Dad and Joel caught up with me, all out of breath.

"Vat happened, Willard?" Dad wanted to know.

I told my father the whole story, sobbing in relief that I hadn't fallen under the cultivators. Dad walked in front of the team, grabbed Ben's bridle, jerked it a few times and yelled at him repeatedly before slapping him across the nose. "Ja, I'm gonna hafta git rid of dat horse before he kills someone."

Old Ben's reputation grew as an outlaw horse that couldn't be ridden. Anyone who fancied himself a cowboy wanted to ride him, but few had the nerve to try. One neighbor, Gene Ludwig, thought he could ride any horse and one day asked Dad if he could take a crack at Old Ben. Dad agreed when Gene said he wouldn't hold my father responsible for any consequences.

The next Sunday afternoon Gene and a friend from Kokomo showed up decked out in shiny cowboy boots, spurs, tight pants with chaps, large cowboy hats, and buckskin shirts. Their spurs jingled when they walked. They wore the kind of clothes I envisioned myself wearing when I became a cowboy.

"We came to ride that horse."

Dad grinned. "O.K. I'd like to see you do dat. Let's go to da barn and git 'im."

Joel and I looked at all that cowboy regalia and thought this is going to be fun to watch. We got a ladder and climbed up on the barn roof for a grandstand view.

Dad led Old Ben out of the barn and held him while Gene saddled the horse. Ben was used to being harnessed, so he didn't fight being saddled. Then Gene grabbed the reins in his left hand, put one foot in the stirrup and, as Dad stepped back, swung up into the saddle.

Old Ben exploded, arching his back, leaping high in the air, and kicking with both hind feet. He crow-hopped, reared, and bucked around in circles, trying to rid himself of the weight on his back. Gene was trying to stay on, but there was often a lot of air between the sitter and the saddle. Joel and I were transfixed as we watched Old Ben twist, turn, and buck in ways we had never seen before.

Gene was still in the saddle a few seconds later when Old Ben bucked around the corner of the barn toward a big ravine. Joel and I ran to look over the edge of the barn roof. When he got to that big gully, Old Ben gave a mighty leap, clearing the ravine and sending Gene flying into space. Gene landed in the bottom of the ditch, flat on his back. He didn't move for a minute.

"I think he's really hurt!" Joel said.

Then Gene slowly raised his head, rolled over, and got to his feet. He crawled out of the gully and limped back to where Dad stood holding Ben. Gene's new cowboy clothes and boots were scuffed up and he had a hole in the rear of his pants. Dad wanted to know if he was hurt. "Well, I don't feel too good. Kinda sprained my ankle. Man, that horse of yours sure can buck!"

Dad chuckled. "I told ya, no one has ridden 'im yet. You stayed on longer den most of da others."

He invited Gene to try again.

"No, I think I'd better not. My leg's kinda banged up."

Then Gene turned to his cowboy buddy. "Why don't you give him a go?"

"No, Gene, my boots just don't fit well today. They're too tight."

"I'll be glad to lend you mine. They're a little bigger."

But the young would-be cowboy was plain scared, and declined.

Old Ben retained his reputation as the horse no one could ride. Despite all the frustrations he caused us, Dad had considerable pride in owning such a horse.

Old Ben was nearly twenty years old during my last year on the farm, but he remained a rebellious outlaw and continued to run away whenever he got the opportunity. After each hazardous incident Dad threatened to get rid of the horse, but he didn't. I think Ben was a challenge to Dad just as I was in my last years on the farm, and he didn't like to give up on such challenges. A few months after I left the farm, Mother wrote and informed me that Dad had finally sold Old Ben. Thus was he relieved of two challenging individuals in the same year.

19

THE HARTMAN PLACE

We had lived on the Smith farm for only three years when our neighbor George Ehrman bought it. Thus my parents had no choice but to look for another place to rent. I hated the thought of moving and was filled with anxiety. I had learned to love our big brick home tucked in the woods, teeming with wildlife. It gave me a sense of security. I also had many friends at Clay School and did not want to leave them.

The search for a new farm went on for several months; then in January of 1938 my parents announced that they had rented a new farm four miles north of our present home. The new place was also in Clay Township, so we kids would remain in the same public school. I was elated.

The 140-acre property my parents rented was owned by George Morrow, but within a year, Harry Hartman, a nearby neighbor, purchased it for $108 per acre. We always referred to this farm as the Hartman place. We moved in the early spring of 1938, when I was twelve years old. I lived in this rural agricultural environment during my critical teenage years. It helped shape my future.

A large swamp had once covered the center of the farm, but in recent years the government had drained it by digging a deep ditch through the swamp, exposing the fine black organic soil that lay beneath the wetland. The banks of the ditch were overgrown with shrubs, brush, and young trees. Water flowed in the bottom throughout the year. Though narrow, the ditch teemed with wildlife. Many songbirds nested in the vegetation, and groundhogs had numerous burrows along the embankments, which also provided escape holes for cottontail rabbits. Muskrats swam in the waterway and dug their homes into the banks under the water surface. Weasels, opossum, and skunks traveled along the ditch in search of food, while catfish, minnows, frogs, and snakes lived in the water. The artificial waterway was an exciting place for a young naturalist, and I spent many hours tramping along its banks, watching wildlife. The Hartman place had no woods, but I was given permission to use the nearby Poland and Conwell woods, so I had plenty of places to pursue my interest in nature. The big ditch also served as my escape hatch when I clashed with my parents or had other problems in my youth. I often wandered here alone in deep thought, contemplating my problems and my future; it was here that I made some of the critical decisions that directed the course of my life.

The Hartman place

    The buildings on the Hartman place were connected to the main county road by a long lane. Soon after we moved, I built two dozen bluebird boxes and nailed them to the fence posts. In a couple of years the bluebird population exploded, and they serenaded us with warbling songs whenever we walked the lane. This was my first successful environmental effort, and I was proud of my achievement.

    The house was originally constructed of hand-hewn logs, but when we moved there the outside walls were covered with boards. The inside had been plastered, painted, and wallpapered. The thick walls were supposed to keep the house cool in the summer and warm in the winter, but that is not how I remember it. Joel and I slept upstairs in an unheated bedroom. During prolonged cold winter periods, our room was as cold as an icicle. Frost often formed on the inside of the windows, and we crawled under the thick blankets, shivering until our body heat warmed the bedding. In the hot days of August the heat drove us out of the bedroom. We slept on the lawn on top of a thin blanket for days at a time, as it was the coolest spot we could find.

The Hartman place had a combination well house and cool room attached to the kitchen end of the house. There was a huge two-story barn that housed our dairy herd, horses, a small grain bin, and a large haymow. The complex also included a hog barn, chicken house, combination granary and implement shed, a milk house, and a garage. The latter building contained a 32-volt light plant with a bank of batteries. After enjoying electricity for two years we were again without it, except for what we generated with the 32-volt system. We ran the light plant only in the evening while doing the chores and supplemented the system with kerosene lights.

My father liked Harry Hartman, the landlord, and our families became good friends. The Hartmans lived one mile south of us and owned several big farms. They had five children; the three boys, Leonard, Harold, and Glen, were my age or a little younger. We worked together on many farm projects such as haying and threshing. The Hartman boys, my brother Joel, and I also played together whenever we had time, which was usually on Sunday afternoons.

My parents rented the farm on a 50-50 basis. The renter supplied the farm equipment and the labor; the proceeds from the farm were split with the owner. About once a month we had a settling-up. Dad and Mr. Hartman would go over the proceeds for the period and divide the costs and incomes from the farm. Dad considered Harry a fine, generous man. When they divided the income and it came down to splitting a penny, Mr. Hartman always gave the penny to Dad. This was very important to my father.

The settling-up always amounted to a social evening between the two families. We hand-cranked a freezer of ice cream and Mother baked several pies. The ladies visited and we kids played while Mr. Hartman and Dad went over the accounts. During breaks in these activities we filled our stomachs with the desserts.

Besides the Hartmans, we had many other neighbors. The Grahams lived just to the west of us and had twelve children. Many of them were the same age as my brothers and sisters and we got together often. Down the road another mile were the Metcalfs with thirteen children, and then there were the Polands and Creasons each with four to six offspring. Needless to say, the neighborhood filled the school bus in a hurry.

We did have one bachelor neighbor, Ruddy Elkins, who lived with his elderly parents just north of us. They had a small farm of forty acres that Ruddy worked with horses and mules. The family was quite poor. Ruddy could neither read nor write, but he was a hard worker and managed to support his parents.

One of my favorite neighbors was Charley Conwell. He lived near the end of our lane and his house sat next to an intersection of two county roads. Charley was in his early seventies when we moved to the Hartman place. He lived with his older daughter Daisy, who never got married; she stayed home to take care of Papa, probably because her father discouraged any suitors. He was retired but got up at four o'clock every morning. In the summertime, right after chores and breakfast, he sat in a chair on the lawn, smoked his pipe, and watched the cars go by.

I sometimes rode my bicycle over to visit him in the evening. He told me about how things were in the neighborhood in his younger days. Charley remembered when the center of our farm was a big swamp.

"Willard, you cain't believe the ducks dat lived in the big swamp. Sometimes dey block out da sun when dey jumps from the water. Dere were tousands, and dere was a covey of quail on evera five acres. I usta kill a big wash pan full evera week ta eat. Oh, dere was 'coons, rabbits, rats (muskrats), and deer. Dere was wildt things everawhere."

I was fascinated by his description of the past, when half the county was still woods and the area was teeming with even more wildlife.

"It warn't all good; dere wore skeeters everawhere. You can haf da good ol' days."

I visited him often and never got enough of his tales, even though I surmised he exaggerated a bit. Sometimes we sat in silence for long periods while he puffed on his pipe, just an old man and a young boy enjoying each other's company.

He also taught me how to call cock bobwhite quail in the spring. They sat on the fence posts and shrilly called "Bobwhite, bobwhite," trying to attract a mate. Charley would give the low female answering call and sometimes trick them into crossing the road and coming into the yard just a few feet in front of us. We watched quietly as they strutted around looking for a mate.

Charley had very pronounced habits. Besides getting up at 4 A.M. every morning, at 2 P.M. he got into his car and made the four-mile journey to Dusty's Tavern in Galveston where he had a couple of beers. I told my mother about this.

"Yes, Charley's a nice old man, but he smokes and drinks beer and that's not nice. Now just remember, Willard, drinking and smoking are sins, and I don't want you to do those things when you grow up. If you do, the devil will get you."

But I liked old Charley and continued to go over and listen to his stories. Just before eight o'clock, I knew it was time to climb on my bicycle and go home. Charley went into the house then to listen to Gabriel Heater's news commentary on the radio. When that was over, Charley went to bed. The next day he would repeat the ritual.

Galveston was a farmer's town. Besides the tavern it had a grain elevator, hardware store, several implement dealers, a bank, a veterinary, a doctor's office, and other essential services. The local barber was Mr. Oldfather. He was an eccentric fellow who did not believe in unions. Barbers in Kokomo and other nearby towns charged thirty-five cents for a haircut. But when you walked into Mr. Oldfather's barbershop, there was a big sign on the wall: *Every day is Xmas. I do not charge.* That was how he avoided the union. It was common knowledge, however, that all clients were expected to contribute ten cents to Mr. Oldfather after each haircut. About once a month Dad took us boys there in the evening after supper. The shop was always full with other farmers waiting their turn, so Dad could socialize and talk corn and hogs while waiting for a haircut. Most of Mr. Oldfather's business was conducted in the evening, so I doubt that he got home for dinner with his family very often.

The Hartman place was typical of most farms in central Indiana. The neighborhood was a good place to grow up. The hard farm work and the strong family ethics instilled good moral character in the younger generation. This was my environment until I got out into the wider world.

The family, minus Dad, dressed up for church about 1943.
From left: *Joel pulling the camera trigger with a string, Miriam, Omar, Almeda, Mom (Katie Troyer), Sylvia, Philip, and Will*

20

SPRING ON THE FARM

Spring was the rhythmic beginning of another year on the farm and the start of another cycle of the seasons. It was my favorite time of the year as I helped plant the crops and take care of the newly born animals. After a long winter, I looked forward to this period when the sun rose higher in the sky, warming the soil. Soon the drab landscape began to take on a green sheen. Then one day the first flock of geese passed overhead in their V formation. Their northward flight always brought out my wanderlust tendencies as I stood in the barnyard watching them pass, wishing I could follow.

New plants rose from the ground and the trees began to bud. Soon the yellow daffodils, dandelions, and the pink and white blossoms of the fruit trees and shrubs added an array of color to the countryside. Robins and bluebirds arrived, reveling in the new season with their cheery warbling songs while the shrill whistle of the bobwhite quail erupted from the fields, forests, and brushy swales.

As soon as the lawn was covered with green grass, we kids begged Mom to let us take off our shoes. The fresh green grass felt good under our bare feet and between our toes. Without the extra weight, we ran like the wind, leapt and jumped in joyous celebration. In a few weeks our feet became callused, and we ran over gravel paths without feeling any pain. Our parents encouraged us to go barefoot because it saved money on shoes.

I remember one spring I was running across the lawn when suddenly my bare feet felt something cold and clammy. I jumped four feet into the air, screamed, "Snake! Snake!" and ran for the house.

"Mom, there's a snake in the yard!"

For some reason we were scared to death of all snakes.

Mom dropped her cooking pan, ran out the door, and grabbed a hoe.

I pointed out the little reptile, and she dispatched the harmless garter snake with one swipe of the hoe, then threw it to the hogs to eat.

I walked back to the house, put on my shoes, and wore them for a few days until I forgot about the snake.

On spring Sundays after church, I often wandered along the big dredged ditch to see how many muskrats had survived the winter, for I was already anticipating the coming trapping season. I occasionally surprised a cottontail in a brushy thicket and checked groundhog burrows to see if there were any fresh diggings. Birds were already defending territories, and I got excited when I saw my first yellowthroat, song sparrow, or brown thrasher. The bullfrogs were croaking, and sometimes Joel and I went out at night with flashlights to catch a few to eat.

Spring was a busy time on the farm—suddenly everything needed doing. One of the first jobs was to haul the tons of manure that had accumulated during the long winter and spread it on the fields. Big piles of it lay behind the milking parlor, and several feet of it covered the floor of the cattle shed, horse barn, and hog house.

Saturdays were manure days in the early spring for Joel and me. As soon as we finished eating our oatmeal and johnnycakes spread with thick apple butter, we put on our knee boots and headed for the barn. We harnessed Cory and Old Ben and hitched them to the manure spreader.

The manure had been tromped over all winter, and we had to work hard with pitchforks to loosen it and heave it into the spreader. When the load was full, I climbed onto the seat and urged the horses forward. They were eager to work, prancing and snuffling as I drove them to the field. I put the manure spreader in gear. The sprocket wheel whirred, tearing the rich organic wastes into small pieces, sending them flying into the air. If I were lucky, I wouldn't get hit in the back of the head with a sloppy, smelly clump. When the load was empty, I trotted the team back to the hog shed, and Joel and I forked on another load.

We took turns driving the team and unloading the manure. It was hard work, but I rather enjoyed the physical effort in the morning. By evening, however, I looked forward to Sunday and church, as I knew we would get a reprieve from hauling manure.

As soon as the soil became dry enough to work, usually in early April, it was time to plant oats. They did not require much field preparation. We disked the previous year's cornstalks into the soil and immediately drilled the oats into the ground.

The biggest spring task was plowing all the fields that were to be planted to corn and soybeans. Plowing turned under the soil and buried the manure, as well as the organic residue left from last year's crops. Other farmers in the neighborhood were also plowing from early morning until late evening. I learned to know who was in the field working by the sounds of their tractors. I recognized the steady drone of Charles Graham's Farmall tractor, the constant whine of Charley Conwell's Oliver, and occasionally I could hear the low hum of Lonnie Maddox's Fordson, a mile north of us.

Our country school closed in late April so that we farm kids could go to work in this busy season. Dad often instructed me to start the tractor and get into the field by daylight while the rest of the family did the chores. I was competitive and reveled in the knowledge that in the stillness of the early morning the distinctive putt, putt of our John Deere would announce to the neighbors that I had beaten them to work.

It took a long time to plow a ten-acre field with the John Deere, but I didn't mind as I sang and daydreamed to pass the time. I loved the way spring filled my senses, and at the end of each day I could look at the field and see the progress. I also got satisfaction in knowing our physical efforts would lead to another bountiful harvest at the end of the summer.

By late April the orchards were in full bloom, and the honeybees were busy gathering nectar. In the nearby woods blooming May apples covered the forest floor, and the white blossoms of the wild crab apples and tulip trees shimmered in the sun. Cardinals and orioles were building nests, and the rat-a-tat-tat of the redheaded woodpecker sounded from the large dead snags.

But there was little time for playing or studying nature. My sisters helped Mom plant the garden, do spring cleaning, and care for several hundred baby chicks. Besides plowing the fields, we boys helped with the livestock. We turned the cattle into one of the succulent green fields. The cows had been fed dried hay all winter and were eager for fresh greens. They would rush into the pasture, grabbing a taste here and there, like kids in a candy store.

Once, after letting the cows into the pasture, Joel and I went back and got two calves that had been born that winter. When I released the first calf, it kicked up its heels, ran straight into the fence, and bounced back, falling to the ground. I feared the worst, but the calf jumped up unhurt and ran into the open field.

"Wow!" I said to Joel. "I thought it broke its neck."

"Stand back! I'm gonna let mine go," Joel said.

His calf ran jumping and kicking, but fortunately it raced toward the other calf and away from the fence.

Dad often sent us in search of sows that had wandered off to some remote place to give birth to a litter of pigs instead of using the individual hog house we had provided for them. One day I was sent after a large white pregnant sow. I searched the fields for an hour, then found tracks indicating she had crawled under a fence and escaped into the brush along the large dredged ditch. I followed her tracks carefully for another twenty minutes and finally spotted her nest of grass and leaves under a brushy shrub. I backed up slowly and quietly, then climbed a nearby fence for a better look. She had a large litter of pigs. At that moment she saw me and came bursting out of her nest directly toward me. I leapt over the fence and ran like a scared deer back to the barn to inform my father of the wild mean sow with the new litter.

The month of May was corn-planting time. It symbolized spring more than any other farming ritual; corn was our major crop, and it was critical to get it in the ground on time if we were to get a good crop in the fall. Once the fields were plowed, we disked and harrowed the soil in preparation for planting. On our farm, corn was planted with a two-row corn planter pulled by a team of horses. The planter had two round containers filled with corn kernels that sat above the wheels. In front of the wheels, small shovels opened a shallow furrow into which the kernels were dropped, then covered with soil before being packed down with the wheels.

Nearly all the corn was *checked* (planted in plot intervals of about forty inches) instead of drilled. The steady click, click, click of the corn planter resounded throughout the neighborhood. It was important to keep the rows aligned, so that they were straight, both lengthwise and crosswise. This permitted us to cultivate the corn in both directions, keeping down weeds between the plants. We didn't use herbicides and pesticides to get rid of weeds and bugs in those days, so it was important to keep down the weeds by mechanical means.

After the corn was in the ground, there was no breathing space, for the soybeans and potatoes also needed planting. Soon after that was done, it was time to cultivate the corn.

Corn sprouted and grew rapidly if the weather was warm. When it was about three or four inches high, we cultivated it for the first time.

On the Hartman farm we used a two-row cultivator mounted on the John Deere tractor. Before that, we had used horse-drawn cultivators.

The first cultivation was done very slowly. Usually this tedious task fell to me. The cultivator shovels were adjusted to cut or cover the weeds but not bury the small corn shoots. At 1 mph, it took forever to make one pass through a long field of corn. Once I finished cultivating the field lengthwise, Dad had me repeat the process crosswise. I got rather bored driving the tractor at such a slow pace.

Later, when the corn got several feet high, I put the John Deere into third gear and raced down the corn rows at nearly 5 mph. When I came to the end of the field, I stood up and throttled the tractor back. In a smooth, quick motion, I raised the cultivator shovels, spun the steering wheel, aligned the tractor with the next two rows, and lowered the cultivators into the ground. Dad was always amazed at how fast I turned the corners and praised me for my skill. After completing the turn, I sat down, increased the throttle and sped down the rows again. My eyes remained on the cornrows constantly, because if I veered slightly to the left or right the cultivators cut off the corn instead of the weeds. I liked the fast speed. It didn't get so monotonous and I could complete a ten-acre field in a hurry.

Spring was an exciting time for me as I helped with the crops and the newborn pigs and lambs. I liked the pleasant aroma of the flowers in bloom, and I was thrilled to see and hear the returning birds that had been absent during the long winter. Spring was quite a contrast to the hot summer days to come.

21

HAYMAKING

After all the crops had been planted and the corn cultivated at least once, it was time to make hay. We made hay during the hot summer weather because that was when it became mature for cutting, then dried fast in the hot sun. Most farmers in Indiana raised clover, alfalfa, or timothy hay. My dad raised clover, which produced two crops each season. Like squirrels that spend the fall storing nuts for the winter, we spent the summer filling the barn with tons of dried hay to feed the livestock through the long winter.

By the end of June the clover fields were in bloom. The smell of fresh clover blossoms permeated the air, and every honeybee and bumblebee in the neighborhood was out collecting the sweet nectar. The bobolinks warbled cheerily from the tops of clover plants, while goldfinches perched on the occasional thistle weeds that protruded above the hay field, unaware of the disaster to come. For when the farmers cut the hay, many birds often lost nests they had built in the middle of the field.

Even after we had a tractor we continued to cut hay with a horse-drawn mower, a two-wheeled implement that had a long sickle bar on the right side. To mow, I lowered the bar to within a few inches of the ground. The mower cut a five-foot swath of clover as I drove around the field from outside to inside.

I watched for bird nests as the team moved along. If I spotted a nest in time I stopped the horses, lifted the sickle bar, and drove past the nest before starting to cut again. After I completed a field, patches of standing clover remained where I had saved bird nests. Dad hated to see any hay wasted, but he tolerated my love of birds.

I also watched for baby cottontails scurrying through the clover in front of the sickle. If I saw one in time, I stopped the horses and waited for the little rabbit to run away. Occasionally the sickle did cut or kill one. It always made me sick to have that happen. When I finished mowing an entire field, however, the rabbits had no place to hide. They ran out of the field seeking cover in nearby fencerows.

The cut hay was left lying on the ground for several days to dry in the sun. Dad always worried about rain when a field of hay was down. If the hay got wet too many times, the rain leeched out the nutrients and it had little food value for the livestock. Sometimes during a rainy period, we lost most of the crop. To choose the best time to cut hay, Dad would watch the skies, hope for sunshine and, like many farmers, consult the Farmers Almanac, a calendar that forecast the general weather in advance.

After the cut hay dried, we raked it into rows with a side-delivery rake pulled by a team of horses. This ingenious implement moved forward at an angle. It had large tines that turned in a circular barrel-like fashion and rolled the loose hay into windrows. Once the hay was raked into windrows, we let it dry a little more before we hauled it to the barn for storage.

On the Hartman farm we hooked a hay loader behind a wagon that was pulled by our tractor. The loader, another laborsaving invention of that era, moved the hay from the ground to the top of the wagon. It had a roller that picked up the hay from the ground; then a series of moving prongs fastened to wooden boards gradually shoved the hay to the top of the rear end of the wagon. It was a lot faster and easier than pitching the hay by hand, though we still had to level the hay with pitchforks.

Usually Joel and I were given the task of loading the hay, and for this we put our younger brothers, Omar and Philip, to work. By the time they were five years old we had taught them how to steer the tractor, but they were not strong enough to pull or push the hand clutch on the John Deere. We solved this problem by tying a long rope from the clutch handle to the front of the hay wagon. When we got ready to start loading, one of us pushed the handle forward to engage the clutch, then quickly ran back and climbed on the hay wagon. Omar or Philip steered the tractor over the windrow, while Joel and I forked the hay forward on the wagon as the loader pushed it up to us. It was hard, dirty work. When the hay came up too fast, one of us tromped forward through the loose hay, jerked the rope to the clutch, and stopped the tractor while we leveled the load. When we got ready to proceed, one of us would climb down and push in the clutch again. When the wagon was full we unhooked the hay loader and pulled the wagon to the barn for unloading.

Loading hay on a hot summer day was usually dull work, but I recall one day when it got exciting. Joel and I were forking hay forward as it dropped from the top of the hay loader, when I looked up and saw a snake tumbling down. I shrieked, "Snake! Snake!" and leapt off the ten-foot-high load. Joel saw it and jumped off the opposite side. We stood on the ground wondering what to do, when it slithered out of the hay and dropped to the ground. Joel and I immediately attacked the snake with pitchforks and killed it. The reptile was a medium-sized garter snake and harmless.

Occasionally other small animals hiding under the hay rows got caught in the hay loader and pushed to the top, such as field mice or small rabbits, but they never produced the response the snake did.

Like most barns, ours had a high roof, providing lots of space in the second story for hay. We placed the hay wagon directly under the roof gable in front of the barn, which was equipped with a steel track fastened to the ridgepole. The track extended the full length of the barn and out under the gable. A hayfork attached to the track could be raised and lowered by a series of ropes and pulleys. The fork had four long curved steel prongs which, when set, grabbed the hay like a claw.

Four of us worked together to unload the hay. Typically, Dad would set the fork in the hay, walk to the end of the wagon, and yell, "O.K. Let 'er go!" Then one of our sisters would lead the horse forward. The ropes strained and creaked as the horse pulled the forkful of hay up to the track on the roof. The fork would click into the track, then glide the load of hay back to Joel and me in the haymow. We would pull the fork into the proper position, dump the load, and then yell, "Pull 'er out!" While Dad pulled the fork back for another load, Joel and I rolled and forked the hay into every nook and cranny. Four forkloads usually emptied a hay wagon.

Working in the mow was hard, dirty work. There were no windows in the mow and thus no breeze or fresh air. The summer sun beating on the roof sent temperatures soaring. We were up to our knees in the loose hay, making every step an effort. I often tied a big bandanna around my neck and over my nose to keep out some of the dust, but still it crept in everywhere. Within an hour our shirts were wringing wet from sweat and our bodies covered with grime. When we got done unloading the hay, we went back to the field for another load. We repeated the process all day, day after day after day until the hay crop was stored.

While the work was miserable, using the hayfork was a lot faster and easier than pitching hay into the mow with a pitchfork. Of course haying would have really been easier had my dad used a hay baler as many farmers did, but baling the hay cost more, so he continued to put up loose hay all the while I was growing up on the farm.

By the end of a full day of making hay I was dead tired, but I still had to help with the milking and the other chores. After supper I was ready to collapse into bed, but about then Mother would shout, "Now, Willard and Joel, you get out the tub, roll up your pant legs and wash your dirty feet and legs. I know they're black with dirt."

"Oh, Mom, can't we forget it tonight?" one of us would protest.

"No, boys. You'll get the bed sheets dirty."

They were usually already dirty, but Mother made a big effort to keep things clean, even in the haying season. Sometimes we sneaked into bed without washing our feet, and by the end of a week of haying, the sheets were filthy.

On Saturday night we had to take the big weekly bath to get cleaned up for Sunday. During haying season our sisters absolutely refused to use the tub after Joel and I had bathed unless we washed and cleaned it.

I hated haymaking, but even that miserable task had some bright spots. When Mother sent one of our sisters to the field with a cold jug of lemonade, boy, it tasted good and refreshed our sweaty bodies. Sometimes we worked with the Hartmans making hay. That was a lot more fun. Joel, the Hartman boys, and I played a lot of pranks on each other while working, which made the time go faster. We often got into water fights at the pump or the horse trough during the hot muggy days. Sometimes one or more of us ended up getting thrown into the trough, which cooled us off a bit.

Haymaking was also dangerous at times. I fell off the hay load several times but never got seriously hurt. We had a neighbor who accidentally reached into the mower sickle and lost several fingers. On another occasion Bill Graham, several other neighbors, and I were helping Lonnie Maddox unload hay. It was my job to lead the horse to the hay rope while Lonnie set the fork on the hay wagon. From my position I could not see the hay wagon, but I thought I heard Lonnie yell, "Pull 'er up." I proceeded forward with the horse, then suddenly I heard a scream, "Stop! Stop!" Bill Graham came running around the corner of the barn and yelled for me to back up. "Lonnie's hand's caught in the pulley!"

I was white with fear at those words and quickly backed up, then ran around the corner of the barn. I saw Lonnie holding his hand, blood dripping profusely. The pulley had ripped off some flesh from his hand and crushed several fingers. I felt terrible, since I had caused the accident. We rushed Lonnie to the local doctor in Galveston, and haymaking came to an end for the day. You always had to be on guard against accidents, but they did occasionally happen.

Like many things on the farm, the task of handling hay was never done. During the winter, we pitched the hay down from the mow and forked it into the cow and horse mangers. After they digested it, we pitched their wastes out behind the barn, and then in the spring we again forked the remains into the manure spreader and hauled it back onto the field where the long journey had started.

22

THE SWIMMIN' HOLE

Nearly every farm boy in Indiana had a swimming hole where he could take a dip after a day of working in the hot sun. Joel and I were no exception. When we first moved to the Smith farm, we found several pools in the creek below the house. As they were barely knee-deep, we flailed our arms, kicked, and imagined we were swimming.

The Wildcat Creek swimming hole

A few years later we found a good hole in Wildcat Creek behind Lee Miller's place. It was about a half-mile from the road and hidden by dense woods. The pool was quite large and up to my shoulder in depth. On its edges were several logjams and one big rock. The hole was about the wildest spot we knew of in our neighborhood. We claimed it as our swimmin' hole and kept its whereabouts secret to all but our closest friends.

After we moved to the Hartman farm, Joel and I and the three Hartman boys rode our bikes the four miles to the Ehrmans on Sunday afternoons. Bobby Ehrman joined us and the six of us hiked a half-mile through the woods to the swimming hole. We spent the afternoon diving off the logs and the rock, having water fights, holding contests to see who could stay underwater the longest, playing tag, and chasing each other up and down the creek. We were proud of the fact that we never saw anyone near our isolated pool.

Most of us boys learned to swim in the Wildcat Creek hole. We never took swimming lessons, but by imitating frogs with our mighty kicks and flailing arms, we managed to stay on top of the water and make some forward progress. We leapt from the logs, which we called diving, but we were primarily taking belly busters. Our pool didn't have the cleanest water. The big industrial Kokomo Steel Mill dumped its wastes into Wildcat Creek, making the water rusty for miles. A little rust never bothered us kids, and our mothers encouraged us to swim there because they felt it was safer than one of the local deep gravel pits.

A couple of hours in our secret swimming hole refreshed us for a few days even though our skins took on a slight reddish-brown color. Years later I concluded that the hole remained a big secret because most of the neighborhood mothers never let their kids go near the rusty-colored Wildcat Creek.

About 1940 George Ehrman dug a gravel pit in the small creek below his house. For several summers the pit became a big social gathering area on hot Sunday afternoons. We Troyer kids, the Hartmans, the Rodys, the Ehrmans and many of their cousins congregated at the pit to swim, socialize, and cool off. Sometimes twenty or more people were in the water at one time. George and Eva Ehrman were good hosts; they encouraged us kids to come spend Sunday afternoon at their place, and they participated in our games.

My sisters, Miriam and Sylvia, were good friends with Betty Ehrman, so they and a few other girls joined in the fun. With girls present, we boys had to be on good behavior; there was no swimming in the nude, something we had enjoyed at Wildcat Creek.

This social swimming hole lasted only about three summers. Heavy spring rains washed dirt and sand down the little creek and filled the pit, but about the same year another neighbor, Glen Keisling, dug a huge gravel pit on his property. It was very deep in spots, but by then we all swam with confidence.

The Keisling pit got quite popular and all the boys swam in the nude. You were considered a sissy if you wore a swimming suit. The pit was just far enough from the road so that you could see we were swimming in our birthday suits but you couldn't see any details. A bunch of boys cavorting in the nude was a big red flag to any decent girl, so the Keisling pit remained a strictly stag swimming hole.

Some of us boys hauled in a big wooden plank, stuck one end into the bank, and spiked it down. It protruded over the water about ten feet and was about eight feet above the surface. By jumping up and down on the end of the board, we managed to get some spring out of it and learned how to dive. We practiced doing half gainers like competitive divers, but most of our dives ended in big belly flops.

The Keisling pit was about four miles from our farm. After a hot, dusty day of haying or threshing, the Hartman boys and we sometimes rode our bikes over after supper. After a cool refreshing swim we pedaled home in the dark.

Spring always brought a race to see who would be the first to take a swim. Some brave soul usually jumped in by the end of March, when the water was icy cold. Usually a few of us stood on the bank daring each other to follow.

"Let's jump in."

"No, it's too cold. Are you crazy?"

"Oh, come on, sissy, I'm goin' in," someone would say and start taking off his clothes. Then it was splash, splash, and splash as one by one we followed the leader.

"Whooee! It's cold!" Immediately we were gasping for breath and racing to get out of the water, our skins turning blue. We shivered as we rushed to get dressed, but we wore the proud label of being the first ones to swim that spring.

One summer Joel and I decided to build a small pool for swimming in the dredged ditch on the Hartman farm. We hauled rocks and some old planks down to a narrow part of the ditch and built a dam about three feet high. The next Sunday we decided to try our new pool and invited a few friends to participate. I was the first one in the water and stood on the bottom to show everyone the depth. Everyone was peeling off his clothes to dive in when I saw a big dark water snake crawl out of the dam and into the murky water. "Snake! Snake!" I screamed and rushed to get out of the water.

Suddenly everyone lost interest in trying the new pool. Probing the dam with some long sticks, we flushed several other snakes into the water. Apparently the reptiles decided our dam was a good hiding place. Even though I loved most wildlife, I had a fear of snakes and hated them. Even a garter snake sent me scurrying. We never again tried to swim in our artificial pool, preferring to bike four miles to the Keisling pit.

Because of our other Sunday obligations, Sunday afternoons were the only time all the neighborhood kids could get together and play. The Mennonite Church service, while shorter than the Amish service, rarely let out before noon. Then we drove the fifteen miles home in the Model A. Even by speeding along at 40 mph, we rarely got home before one o'clock. We usually sat down to eat about 1:30 and finished by 2 P.M. We kids rushed through the meal, but then we had to wait at the table for Dad to finish eating and say a prayer. We raced from the table after the "Amen." We had to be back by 5:30 to do the milking, so the 3½ hours we had to play once a week were precious to us. When we got older, Joel and I were allowed to drive the Model A, which was faster than riding our bikes and gave us more time for recreation.

While we usually swam for summer recreation, we would also play softball, ride bikes, or ride ponies. In winter we sledded on the Bausom Hill or found a frozen pond to play hockey with sticks and a tin can.

If it was too cold to swim but not cold enough for winter sports, we gathered at some neighbor's barn, with a hoop, for a game of basketball. At other times we entertained ourselves in the haymow by doing somersaults or jumping from a high beam into the soft hay. We always found some form of recreation, regardless of the weather. In contrast to our intense physical activity, our parents visited, read, or just rested on Sunday afternoons.

If for some reason my friends couldn't play on Sunday afternoon, I took a stroll through a neighbor's woods or along the big ditch on the Hartman farm, looking for birds. I became quite knowledgeable on Indiana birds and my interest in nature continued to grow. My older sister Almeda, who was working for a family in Kokomo during the week, often went to the library and checked out nature books for me. I read constantly on this subject when I was in my teens.

Occasionally my parents planned a big family outing, such as the time they organized an all-day trip to Brown County State Park with our friends the Wiley Masts. We got up at four o'clock, did the milking, and met the Masts in Kokomo before seven. We then drove the hundred miles to Brown County, which took three hours in our Model A. Six of us kids were jammed in the back seat, while little Phil rode in front with our parents. The trip seemed to take forever, and we entertained ourselves by guessing what make of car was coming in our direction. After numerous pit stops, we made it to the park, where we hiked, played, and explored the woods. I discovered some birds new to me, watched numerous fox squirrels, and spied a raccoon peering out of its hole in a big hickory tree. I was elated and ran back to get Joel. When we returned to the tree, the raccoon was out on a limb with three young ones in tow. "Look at that, Willard!" Joel said. "I'm goin' back to git the rest of the family!"

Soon all of us stood near the tree watching the family of 'coons. The forest was immense, in contrast to the small wood lots at home, and I felt like I was following in Daniel Boone's footsteps. I imagined myself wandering for days in this tree-filled region.

Soon, however, Mother called for all of us to come eat. We found a big maple tree, sat in its shade, and had a picnic of fried chicken, potato salad, bean salad, and several pies for dessert.

We left Brown County in mid-afternoon. Mom drove, and I saw the speedometer creep to 45 mph. Dad caught it and said, "Katy, slow down. You're doin' 45!"

"Yes, I wasn't watchin'. This machine is just runnin' so smooth today."

We got home at 6:30, quickly changed our clothes, and did the milking. It had been a long day, but it was a welcome change from the routine farm life. Brown County was the farthest I got from home until I was eighteen years old. It was like another world to us kids, and we talked about the trip for days.

Another time, we took most of a day off and drove forty miles to visit a blue heron rookery Mother had read about in the paper. I was impressed with the big colony of birds in the trees and watched intently as they fed their young. These were big birds I seldom saw on our farm, and that evening I got out my bird book and read everything on herons. In a subtle way Mother encouraged my interest in nature. She appreciated wildlife and, I think, secretly hoped I would pursue a career in some field of nature, even though she was encouraging me to become a farmer.

Although we had much less time to play or spend with our hobbies than many kids do today, we enjoyed every minute of it. We were never bored with our free time and certainly never lacked for things to do. We always looked forward to those short Sunday afternoons.

23

THRESHING TIME

Threshing (pronounced *thrashing* by most Indiana farmers) was the biggest working social event of the year, involving all our neighbors. It was the highlight of the farm season and, to small farm children, almost as exciting as Christmas. The men and boys, along with some strangers, did the fieldwork while the women and girls prepared the big threshing dinner.

Before the actual threshing occurred in late July, there were many steps involved in harvesting the grain. Once the wheat and oat fields turned from green to golden and the seed heads filled out, it was time to cut the crop. It had to be done after the kernels were plump and filled with protein but before the heads got too dry, shattered, and fell to the ground.

In the past the harvest had been a much more labor-intensive affair. Our ancestors cut the grain with knives or a scythe, then gathered the stalks into clusters called sheaves, stacking them to dry. Men and women carried the sheaves to a granary floor, then beat them with clubs to extract the grain from the chaff. The method was very inefficient and so wasteful that gleaners searched the fields for leftover grain.

By about the mid-1800s, the invention of mechanized equipment made harvesting much more efficient and easier. When I was growing up, nearly all the wheat, oats, and barley were cut with a grain binder. This may seem like an outmoded implement to modern farmers, but at the time it was an ingenious piece of equipment. My dad owned a McCormick-Deering binder, which was pulled by three or four horses and cut a six-foot swath of grain. It had a sickle bar similar to a hay mower that cut the grain about six inches above the ground. Behind the sickle bar was a large flat canvas conveyor belt. A huge turning reel with long horizontal paddles rode above the sickle. The paddles extended out in front of the sickle and gently pushed the top of the grain onto the canvas once it was cut. The turning conveyor belt carried the material to the right, then up and over the large broad wheel under the binder. As it entered the right side, it was bunched into sheaves. Then a roll of twine, which moved through various small pulleys and steel eyes, tied the sheaves into bundles and dropped them onto a carrier fork.

When in operation, all the gears, pulleys, rollers, and chains driven by the single large wheel under the right center of the binder made a lot of noise. When the carrier was full of bundles, the operator, who sat behind the binder on a high seat, tripped the carrier with his foot and dropped the bundles on the ground.

When Dad was almost through cutting a field, Joel and I, as small boys, followed behind on foot and watched for rabbits that were losing their homes in the tall grain and running for cover. We gave chase, and sometimes we managed to catch a small one and hold it for a while before releasing the poor frightened bunny. We even tried to keep a few for pets without much success.

Once the grain was cut and the bundles lay in rows, we put them into shocks. When I was about seven years old, Dad taught me how to shock oats. I took a bundle in each hand, placed the butts on the ground a little ways apart, and pushed the heads together. I added two more at a time until there was a round teepee-shaped shock of eight to ten bundles. I then took one or two sheaves and laid them on top of the shock to form a cap. The caps shed most of the rain and gave some protection against hail. Joel and I would spend several days shocking a ten-acre field. The shocks sat in the field to dry for a week or more before the threshing crew hauled them away. When you saw a field dotted with shocked grain, you knew a threshing would soon take place.

Very few farmers could afford to own their own threshing machines. Usually the machines were owned by cooperatives or by individuals who contracted them out. A group of neighboring farmers arranged to have a threshing machine come to their farms, then pooled their resources to supply the labor and other equipment necessary to do the job. Everyone in the threshing ring contributed something, whether it was themselves with a pitchfork or a team of horses and a wagon to haul shocked grain in from the field.

When we lived on the McGrawsville farm, our father belonged to a large threshing ring for several weeks each summer. In those days an immense steel-wheeled steam engine was used to power the threshing machine. I still remember climbing up on a high fence to watch the steam engine approach, pulling the big thresher behind. I could see and hear it coming a mile away, puffing a big plume of smoke and steam as it moved slowly along the road. As it turned into our lane I would run into the house yelling, "The big engine is comin'! It's turnin' into our lane right now!"

Soon all of us kids would be sitting on the fence watching the big machine creep along at a snail's pace. When it was directly in front of us, the engineer would wave and yell at us, but being bashful, we barely raised our timid little hands to acknowledge him. I would peek out from under my big straw hat in wide-eyed amazement at this huge mechanical monster.

Once the engineer gave us a real thrill by reaching forward and pulling the whistle. The shrill blast almost knocked us off the fence. Then he took his hat off, waved it, and shouted, "How'd ya like dat toot?" Ecstatic, we waved and laughed. As the machine crept toward the barn, Joel and I jumped off the fence and followed behind. When the big engine stopped at the barn, the engineer blew three long blasts on the whistle. This announced to the neighborhood that the threshing rig had arrived at the Troyers.

The next morning, soon after daylight, neighboring farmers came to help with the harvest. Some arrived with teams of horses and wagons, others walked with pitchforks over their shoulders, and a few arrived by buggy or car. People and equipment were everywhere. All this commotion was the most exciting thing a farm kid would experience for an entire year. Soon eight to ten wagons were in the field being quickly loaded with grain bundles by men with pitchforks. Meanwhile, near the barn the engineer and several helpers in greasy overalls got the machine ready. They hooked the steam engine to the thresher with a big wide belt, which was the source of the threshing machine's power. Then they adjusted chains, blowers, screens, conveyor belts, rollers, and numerous other devices that made the machine run and do the work of many men.

When loaded, the wagons headed for the barn. The first wagon was driven alongside the threshing machine, and the driver started tossing grain bundles onto the conveyor belt. Once the conveyor carried the bundles into the separator at regular intervals, grain poured from a spout into a box wagon while the straw shot from a long blower pipe onto a pile. Joel and I would stand about a hundred feet away, watching.

Horses took awhile to get used to the noise of turning wheels, clanking chains, moving cylinders, and the big hissing steam engine. Once we saw a team of young Percherons approach the machine, tossing their heads up and down nervously. The driver urged them forward, but they stopped, reared, neighed, and refused to go closer to the noisy machine. Joel whispered to me, "I think they're goin' to run. Let's git behind that other wagon." But then another driver waiting in line jumped from his wagon, ran forward, grabbed the balking team by their reins, and slowly led them forward.

Joel and I wandered around all day in our big straw hats, watching the entire operation in wide-eyed wonder. It was as exciting as going to a circus, and we hated to see it come to an end. But by late afternoon the crews had hauled in the last load of bundles and tossed them into the machine. Horse-drawn wagons moved down our lane while the engineer and his helpers shut down the machine. They took off the big belt and hitched the steam engine to the thresher. Then they crept out our lane toward the next farm, where the operation would be repeated the next day.

The fields that had been filled with shocked grain for days now stood dramatically empty, all accomplished in a single day. Dad gave a satisfied smile as he looked at his bins full of oats and wheat and the big pile of straw. But his work was not done; tomorrow he would leave soon after daylight with his team and wagon to help another neighbor thresh grain.

By the time we moved to the Hartman place the remaining threshing rings were much smaller. Many farmers harvested grain with a newer invention, the modern combine. The Hartmans, a few other neighbors, and we however, continued the old tradition. Harry Hartman owned a threshing machine and we formed our own small ring from Harry and his three boys (Leonard, Harold, and Glen), Grandpa Hartman and his hired hand Lloyd Cook, us Troyers, and a few others. Usually the Hartman boys' Uncle Fritz from Texas came to help. Our operation consisted of twelve to fifteen men and boys, less than half the size of the old threshing rings.

I was old enough by then to perform the work of a man and no longer served as water boy. That task fell to my younger brothers Omar and Philip. I usually drove one of the bundle wagons, as did Leonard, Harold, and Lloyd. We boys often raced to see who could put on the biggest load and finish first. I liked to drive our big draft horses, Corey and Bell, because they were powerful pullers yet gentle. Unlike Old Ben, they could be trusted to pull as directed and not try to run away.

Threshing time at the Hartmans

To load a wagon I placed the bundles along each outer edge of the wagon bed, butts out, as the pitcher tossed them to me. Then I laid some lengthwise in the middle, covering the heads of the outer bundles to bind everything together. As the pitcher finished a shock, I commanded the horses to move forward to the next shock. Once the load was filled to the top of the wagon racks, I drove the team to the thresher and unloaded it, pitching each individual bundle onto the separator conveyer belt, head first.

Harry ran the threshing machine with an ordinary tractor instead of a big steam engine. He would throttle the tractor back to turn the threshing machine at a steady 800 to 1000 rpm. With our small crew and only four or five bundle wagons, Harry occasionally shut the machine down to await another bundle wagon. The threshed wheat went directly into the Hartman's truck and then much of it was immediately hauled to the grain elevator in Galveston or Kokomo to be sold. One of us boys hauled the grain, a job we competed for as soon as we were sixteen years old and had a driver's license.

The blower attendant had the dustiest and dirtiest job. When we blew the straw into an enclosed shed, someone had to be inside directing the stream of straw. The blower man could hardly see through his goggles as clouds of dust permeated the inside of the shed. The dust penetrated his bib overalls and found its way up his sleeves, pant legs, and inside his shirt. By the time the attendant spent a half-hour in the shed he was covered with dust and itching from all the chaff. But being dirty during threshing was a badge of honor that showed you were not afraid of hard work.

At noon we shut down the operation to have a big feed. Mom, Mrs. Hartman, and some of my sisters had spent hours preparing our midday dinner. After working, everyone was famished and ready for the feast. First, we tried to clean up a bit. We brushed each other off with a broom, then we lined up at the well. One of us pumped the handle while the rest of us took turns sticking our heads under the stream of cool water and splashed it over our faces and arms to wash away the worst of the filth.

Once we were half-clean, we sat down around the big threshing table and helped ourselves to the mounds of food. We would have fried chicken, roast beef or pork, mashed potatoes, gravy, fresh corn, tomatoes, peas, applesauce, a couple of casseroles, bean salad, biscuits, jams, and relishes. Dessert amounted to several kinds of pies, perhaps a peanut-banana pudding, and sometimes ice cream. We gorged until our stomachs hurt, then went outside and lay under a shade tree for a half-hour to let our meals settle.

"O.K. boys, it's time to go back to work," came the call from Harry.

We groaned but staggered to our feet and headed for the barn. Soon we were back in the field with our bundle wagons and before long, the threshing machine was humming again as we tossed in the bundles of oats or wheat. The work continued until about six o'clock, then we trotted our teams home and did the chores.

Threshing days were laboriously long, but I enjoyed the camaraderie of working with neighbors and friends. It made the time go faster and I looked forward to each day. We boys often played tricks on each other, such as unhooking the horse traces from the wagon when the driver wasn't looking. When the driver directed his team forward, they moved without the wagon. If you stood too close to a big livestock water tank, you might find yourself tossed in by several of your friends.

Sometimes the Hartman boys and we rode our bikes to the Keisling pit in the evening for a refreshing dip, which got rid of the itchy chaff and dirt from threshing. Many days, however, Joel and I were forced to get out the tub and wash the worst of the grime from our legs before we went to bed. After a short night's sleep, we were ready for another day of hard physical labor.

Threshing in our small ring lasted only about one week, and I hated to see this communal project come to an end. I always looked forward to threshing time the following year.

24

THE FALL HARVEST

Fall brought relief from the scorching summer temperatures. As the days got shorter, the nights turned frosty and the leaves of the maples, oaks, and other hardwood trees changed the green landscape to crimson and gold. The bluebirds, bobolinks, and robins left for southern climates, and flocks of geese again winged overhead in their V formations, this time heading south. Fall also brought the harvest of all the crops that remained in the fields and garden.

Mom and my sisters had been canning all summer, lining the cellar with hundreds of jars filled with green beans, peas, corn, tomatoes, beets, pickles, plums, peaches, pears, strawberries, and raspberries. Several large crocks of sauerkraut sat in the corner. Now it was time to pick the late apples and to make applesauce, cider, and the last batch of apple butter. The big yellow pumpkins were ripe, and Mother canned a large supply so we could enjoy pumpkin pies all winter. We also hauled a wagonload or two to the barn. These we sliced apart with a long machete and fed to the cows at milking time. We stored at least three dozen of the big white-necked squash in the root cellar to keep us supplied with our favorite fall breakfast: fried squash with tomato gravy.

The late potatoes and onions were dug and put in a big bin in the dark cool root cellar to keep them firm all winter. One bin was also filled with fall apples. The last tomatoes, which had been nipped by frost, were a bit mushy but would be gathered and cooked into many bottles of ketchup. Once the cellar was full, we knew there would be plenty of food to last the family all winter.

In the barn the haymow and the straw sheds were stuffed, and the grain bins were filled with wheat and oats. We had combined the ten- or fifteen-acre field of soybeans in early fall and sold most of the beans. But then we faced one of the biggest events of the year, the corn harvest.

Corn was the primary field crop on our farm as it was throughout the region. We dedicated nearly a third of the farm acreage to raising this crop. It was our main source of livestock feed; each year we fed several thousand bushels to our hogs, cows, horses, and chickens. Prior to the introduction of hybrid corn in the late 1930s, a farmer was lucky to get sixty bushels of corn per acre. With the hybrids and better farming practices, good land could produce a hundred bushels per acre.

Most of the corn was left in the field to mature and dry before it was harvested. After we moved to the Hartman Place, we used four or five acres to fill the farm's big round silo with silage. Silage utilized the whole corn plant-stalk—ears and all—while it was still green and full of moisture. Dad always planted a field of corn mixed with sorghum for this purpose. The sorghum plant was a little sweeter and juicier than corn, adding a little flavor for the cattle.

We cut the corn and sorghum with a corn binder. The machine sliced the plants off near the ground and tied them into bundles. Then we hauled the bundles to the silo with our horses and wagons. A silage chopper, powered by the tractor, chopped the corn and sorghum into fine pieces and blew the silage into the forty-foot silo.

Silo filling was a communal project like grain threshing, though it took fewer people and less time. We, with the Hartmans and the Grahams, worked together to fill each other's silo. The juices and sugars of the green silage partially fermented when packed into this round storage bin and resulted in a preserved animal feed that would keep all winter. Dad often sent me into the silo to tramp down the fresh chopped greens so they would ferment faster. The cows loved it, preferring it to dry hay.

The first time our silo was filled, Joel and I learned that fermented silage produces a little alcohol. After the silage sat for a few days, some juice seeped out of the bottom of the silo, forming a small pool of liquid on the ground. I was feeding the cows in the barn when Joel yelled, "Hey, Willard, come 'ere. I got somethin' to show ya."

Walking around the corner of the barn, I saw Joel standing by the silo, watching a dozen chickens drink the silage liquid.

"Look! They're drunk!" Joel said with a laugh. Sure enough, the chickens were staggering around in a drunken stupor. One big rooster tried to crow, but when he stretched out his neck he fell over backward. Some hens leaned over to drink and fell into the pool. Joel and I whooped and laughed at the comical chickens. That evening at supper we related the episode to the family. Everyone thought it was funny, but my folks didn't miss this opportunity to give us a lecture about the evils of alcohol.

Unloading at the silo

By the middle of October the corn was ready for harvest. During most of my time on the farm, we harvested corn by hand and stored it on the cob in well-ventilated corncribs. We shelled corn later as it was needed.

We shucked corn by removing the husks, snapping the ear from the stalk and tossing it into a wagon. A well-trained team of horses pulled the wagon ahead a few steps at a time on verbal command, so that the wagon was almost always directly opposite the corn husker. You always knew where the wagon was and didn't have to look each time you tossed an ear. The far side of the wagon was higher to catch any ears that were thrown a bit too high.

To aid in removing the husk, shuckers wore a peg or hook. We small kids wore a peg on our fingers and jabbed the small metal point under the husk and ripped it open. Then we peeled back the husk, snapped off the ear and tossed it onto the wagon. Older corn huskers wore a hook strapped to the palm of their hands. They grabbed the ear with the left hand and, with the right hand, ripped the hook across the husk to open up the ear. Then they removed the rest of the husk, snapped off the ear, and threw it into the wagon. This was all accomplished in one smooth motion. A good corn shucker could keep an ear in the air almost constantly.

My dad used to say a fast corn husker could shuck an acre a day. So a farmer who had forty acres of corn would spend at least forty days harvesting the crop unless he had kids or a hired hand to help. Since school was in session we were required to help only on Saturdays. As small kids, we got rather bored and slowed down at times. To motivate us, Dad would promise us a prize at the end of the season.

"Now, if ya kids verk real hard and we git done by Thanksgiving, I'll buy y'all a nickel candy bar."

Thinking about that big candy bar would get us working like beavers for a few hours. But after a while our efforts slowed, and Dad would have to remind us of the potential prize again.

People considered corn husking an art, and public corn husking contests were popular. Corn huskers competed in county and state contests, with the state winners vying for the National Corn Husking Championship. The big event received a lot of media attention every fall in the Midwestern states. Farmers traveled for hundreds of miles to witness the contest. The Kokomo Tribune featured the winner and the details of his husking abilities. All the corn farmers knew his name and, if he won several years in a row, the champion corn husker's name became a household word throughout the corn belt region, similar to some of today's famous athletes.

I had a high school agriculture teacher, Mr. Schwartz, who helped organize an Indiana youth corn husking contest and encouraged me to enter. I considered myself a fairly fast shucker, so I agreed to compete in the county contest. All the entrants shucked for one hour, and when the corn was weighed, a neighbor of ours Walter Creason and I tied for first place. That put Mr. Schwartz in a bind, so Walter and I agreed to flip a coin. I lost. Walter then competed in the state youth contest and came in second. I always wondered if I might have won, had I managed to shuck but one more ear in our local county rivalry. Of course my parents, brothers, and sisters were extremely proud that I came close to winning.

By the early 1940s some of our neighbors got mechanical corn pickers. A man and a couple of boys could harvest a ten-acre field of corn in a day with a two-row corn picker. But Dad, always slow in accepting new ideas and changes, did not work out a deal with a neighbor to harvest our corn crop with a mechanical picker until my last few years on the farm.

Harvesting corn by hand took a long time, a task that lasted well into November. Eventually the last load was husked and shoveled into the corncrib. This came as a welcome relief, because that meant the harvest was complete and we could relax a little. We boys could do some hunting and playing, and Dad could enjoy his favorite pastime—going to farm sales.

During the winter we fed all the grain, silage, and hay to the livestock, and by spring the bins and haymow would be nearly empty again. Then it would be time to start the spring plowing and planting, and the cycle of the seasons would be repeated.

25

HALLOWEENING

Among Indiana farm boys, the tradition of playing Halloween pranks on your neighbors went back several generations. It was considered a part of growing up. I never heard the phrase *trick or treat*. All we did was trick. Farmers accepted the pranks with good humor since, as boys, most had also participated in the sport. In fact, many of our ideas came from our fathers, who related their youthful episodes with some pride.

My pious father told me how he once helped take a neighbor's wagon apart piece by piece, whereupon he and his friends hauled it to the top of the man's barn with ropes and reassembled it. The next morning poor John found his wagon on top of his barn. Farmers came from all over the countryside to look at the barn with the wagon on the roof.

"Sure is a nice weather vane you got on your barn!" one neighbor reportedly teased him.

John grinned at all the kidding and rather enjoyed his celebrity status for a few days. Then he and some neighbors, and probably a few of the culprits, took it apart and let it back down, one piece at a time. People in the area considered it the best Halloween prank of the year.

While Halloween was our impetus, we never confined our tricks to Halloween night. All of October was considered fair game, though we became more active as Halloween night approached. We made secret plans at school; then after finishing our chores and supper, we roamed the neighborhood performing pranks under cover of darkness. As small kids we sneaked through the fields to a neighbor's house and pressed a notched wooden sewing spool against a windowpane, then spun it rapidly with a string. The sound reverberated through the house. We escaped into the darkness, stifling our laughter before the neighbor opened the door.

As we got older and acquired bicycles, then eventually cars, we roamed beyond our immediate neighborhood.

Bill Graham, Russell Moss, and I once decided to smoke out old Charley Conwell. We knew Charley's habits and decided the best time to do the deed was eight o'clock in the evening, while he listened to Gabriel Heater on the radio. The sound of the radio muted our noise on the roof. The nights were chilly in late October, and Charley always kept a coal fire in his pot-bellied stove. We brought a long ladder and leaned it against the house, then one of us stood watch while the other two quietly crept up on the roof and covered the top of the chimney with a board. We fled behind the barn to watch the results. In a few minutes Charley came staggering out the door in a cloud of smoke, coughing and cussing.

"Ya little rascals, whoever ya are. I'll gitcha for dis!"

While we giggled up a storm behind the barn, he spotted the ladder and sent his daughter Daisy up on the roof to remove the board.

Cows were often the focus of our pranks. On several occasions we switched cows between neighbors. We chose two neighboring farmers with cows in a field that had a gate access to the road. We herded the cows from the first field to the second, then took the cows from the second field and ran them back to where we'd found the first ones. It took several boys to make the switch. At other times we simply slipped a halter on several cows and led them to another farm. The next morning when the farmers got ready to milk, they usually recognized the neighbor's cows and switched them back.

We also painted a few cows. If a farmer had a herd of brown Jerseys, we would catch a few and paint stripes and spots on them until they resembled black and white Holsteins. Eventually the paint wore off, but the prank was good for a lot of laughs.

Several of us once put horse harnesses on two dairy cows and hitched them together. When the farmer opened the door to let the cows into the dairy barn the next morning, the two got stuck in the doorway. The farmer had to unharness the cows to get them inside the milking parlor.

We also used crops in our pranks. A common shenanigan was to block a local gravel road with several wagonloads of pumpkins gathered from the nearby fields. Any driver who wasn't alert at night smashed into the pile before he or she could stop.

One morning, during my fifth grade year at Clay school, we found a fodder shock sitting in the middle of the room on top of our desks. The big boys had apparently gotten hold of a key to the school and carried out the mischievous act. Everyone thought the janitor had collaborated by lending them a key, but he swore innocence. Our teacher Mr. Hartman didn't think it was funny, but every kid in school did.

Our parents expected us to have fun but warned us not to be destructive. Once, though, we accidentally slipped over that line. David Haynes, Keith Wright, Rex Dyar, and I were Halloweening one night and decided to scare people with a lot of noise. We gathered several bushels of ear corn, then selected various neighbors' houses with open porches. Each of us grabbed two or three ears of corn, and then we threw them onto the porch so they ricocheted off the walls making an awful clatter. By the time the man of the house stepped outside to investigate, we boys were down the road and out of sight. We hit a number of homes that night; then about midnight we selected a stranger's home near Kokomo. We all hit the porch with our ears of corn, but David miscalculated and one of his ears went through a window, shattering the glass!

"Oh my god! Let's git outta here!" one of my partners said.

We ran clear out of the neighborhood before stopping. We felt bad enough about what we'd done to quit Halloweening for the evening. For several days I was afraid a policeman might come knocking on our door, but my parents never learned of the incident.

Chicken stealing was common in our area, so farmers were always alert to squawking chickens at night. Some even kept shotguns handy. Despite this danger, occasionally we slipped into a neighbor's henhouse and tied long strings to several chickens' legs. Then we unrolled the string to a good hiding place. Once hidden we pulled on the chicken's legs to make them squawk. Often we couldn't wake the farmer, but occasionally we succeeded, especially if old Rover started barking. When the farmer came out the door with his shotgun we fled, trying not to giggle too loudly. As soon as he found the long strings, the farmer knew he'd been Halloweened.

When playing pranks we picked on the young as well as the old. Lovers often parked their cars on remote country roads to do their sparking. A few of us conceived the idea of "rotten tomatoing" them during Halloween season. By mid-October the only tomatoes left in the fields were mushy and putrid, having been frozen several times. We gathered buckets of the decomposed tomatoes, then cruised the backcountry roads in a pickup with the lights off, looking for the lovers. Several of us stood in the back with the rotten tomatoes while an accomplice drove. When we spotted a parked car facing us, we slowly cruised by and dumped a bucket of tomatoes on their windshield. Then we sped down the road, disappearing long before the parked couple could get their clothes on, jump in the front seat, turn the car around and give chase.

Perhaps our favorite Halloween trick in the early 1940s was upsetting outdoor toilets. We knew which neighbors still had them and each season selected some to push over. If they didn't have indoor toilets, they had to use the barn or chicken house until the toilet was raised again. Sometimes we got five or six in one night and often overturned an outhouse that had been toppled the previous year. Some farmers were getting indoor plumbing about that time, so many of the outhouses we pushed over never got erected again.

Upsetting toilets was a stinky mess, but that was all part of the fun. One of the Barker boys in our school accidentally fell in the hole while pushing over an outhouse. He reeked, so the other guys forced him to ride the front fender for the rest of the night. The story made the rounds in school the next day, and we rated it the best Halloween accident of the season.

Once when I was eighteen years old and had acquired a '36 Chevy, several of us boys were using it to cruise the neighborhood looking for outhouse candidates. We decided to hit Sumner Miller's place, which was on a remote country road. Seeing no lights in the house, we left the Chevy on the side of the road and climbed a fence to shove over the toilet. Preoccupied with our prank, we didn't notice a car approaching until it was too late. We hid, hoping the car would pass, but it was Sumner and his wife returning from town. Now, Sumner, having shoved over many an outhouse in his youth, immediately knew what was going on and recognized my car. About then I remembered I had left the keys in the Chevy. Sumner got into the vehicle and drove off, leaving us boys stranded. He had turned the prank on us, and we ended up walking several miles to pick up another car.

We cruised the neighborhood looking for my Chevy but couldn't find it. Sumner had hidden it well and though I searched for several days, I still couldn't find my car. Finally, the day after Halloween, it suddenly appeared in our driveway. My brother Joel worked for

Sumner at that time and knew the secret, but he never revealed where Sumner had hidden the car. To Sumner that was the best Halloween joke of the year, but it wasn't for me.

26

THE WILDLIFE HARVEST

Hunting and trapping were as natural to a farm boy as raising livestock for food and profit. We had a close relationship with our farm animals. We cared for them and made pets of many, but we knew the ultimate goal was to sell them for profit or butcher them for the table. We looked at wild animals in the same manner; they were there for our enjoyment but also for our use. A pair of fox squirrels or cottontail rabbits made a meal for the family, who appreciated the change from our standard fare of chicken, beef, or pork.

Dad was not much of a hunter, but at an early age Joel and I developed an urge to go after wildlife. Dad owned a single-shot, 16-gauge shotgun and occasionally Joel and I talked him into taking us hunting for squirrels and rabbits before we were old enough to carry a gun.

I made my first rabbit hunt when I was only six or seven years old. One morning, after a six-inch snowfall, I spotted fresh rabbit tracks in the orchard. I followed them around the fruit trees and into a nearby cornfield. I saw where the bunny had found and eaten an ear of corn. The tracks continued on, leading me in a big circle before I spotted the cottontail sitting under a broken cornstalk about ten feet away. I stopped and watched it for several minutes. It did not move, so I cautiously backed up one step at a time, until I was about fifty feet away. Then I turned around and slowly walked away. I climbed over the cornfield fence and ran back to the house.

"Dad, Dad, come quick! I found a rabbit sittin' in the deep snow."

"*Wo ist es*? (Where is it?)"

"In the cornfield. Git the gun!"

Seeing my excitement, Dad grabbed his shotgun and followed me. I retraced my steps and, when I was about thirty feet away, I pointed toward the rabbit.

"See 'im sittin' under the cornstalk?" I whispered.

Dad nodded, then slowly moved forward a few more steps. The bunny remained frozen in its hiding place. Dad raised the gun to shoot but then lowered it. Always one to save a few cents, he took the shell out of the gun and crept forward until he was within five feet of his quarry. He slowly raised the gun over his shoulder, then quickly swung, hitting the rabbit over the head, killing it instantly.

I was elated and ran forward to claim the prize, but Dad was moaning, "I broke my gun." Sure enough, the gun had glanced off the rabbit and hit the frozen ground, breaking a steel plate near the trigger. He did save the cost of a three-cent shell, but my father later paid fifty cents to get the gun fixed!

Unconcerned about the broken gun, I rushed back to the house to show Mother the cottontail. She praised my first hunting efforts and cooked a special dinner of rabbit in my honor.

I was about ten years old the first time Dad let me carry a gun to go hunting. Four of us were shucking corn on the Smith farm. A neighbor who liked to hunt was helping us, so Dad had put the shotgun in the back of the wagon in case we saw a rabbit. We spotted several cottontails darting through the cornrows, and each time, Joel or the neighbor took the shotgun and pursued them without success. Finally I asked Dad if I could try.

"Vell, O.K. no vun else is gettin' any," he said.

I sneaked through the cornfield while tightly clutching the gun. Several bunnies hopped across the rows, but they were running too fast for me to shoot. In desperation I whistled sharply at the next rabbit. I was quite surprised when it stopped, sat up, and looked at me. I snapped the gun to my shoulder and fired, killing it. I was elated with my prey and started back, but before I found the others, another cottontail ran down the cornrow. Again my whistle stopped the bunny in its tracks. I proudly carried the two rabbits back to the wagon. Joel saw me coming. "We heard ya shoot. Any luck?"

I grinned and held up the two bunnies. Joel and the neighbor stared in disbelief as I related how I'd tricked the rabbits. Dad was proud of my achievement.

"Now we haff a hunter in da family."

By the time I was twelve, I had saved enough money to buy a .410 gauge, bolt-action shotgun. Joel had also saved his money and purchased a 20-gauge. We became avid hunters, often getting up before daylight to hunt squirrels in a neighbor's woods, just as the morning light was filtering through the trees. We learned to listen for squirrels cracking nuts, then creep quietly toward our quarry. Sometimes we were successful, and if we got two we had enough for a meal. We then rushed home to do the chores and milking. Mother rolled the dressed squirrels in flour, fried them, and made a delicious gravy from the drippings. The entire family enjoyed the treat.

In the fall after the corn harvest, Dad often gave us part of Saturday off to hunt. He considered rabbits and squirrels part of the farm crop. Joel and I roamed the fields and woods hunting squirrels and cottontail rabbits for the table. Any wild animals we killed meant fewer chickens to butcher, leaving more chickens for us to sell.

Dad encouraged us to hunt crows because they ate corn and other grain. Joel and I learned how to make decoys, imitate their calls, and lure the crows within range of our shotguns. Dad also bought us a .22 rifle so we could shoot the numerous starlings and English sparrows that invaded our barn lot and ate grain. We became good shots and could kill a starling a hundred feet away with some consistency.

The more we hunted the more we enjoyed the chase. After moving to the Hartman place we saw an advertisement for Sports Afield Magazine and sent for a year's subscription. We were both eager to read each issue, so when it came each month, we sat together on a chair reading the hunting and fishing articles.

We also became avid trappers. The big ditch that ran through the Hartman farm provided excellent habitat for muskrats and other fur-bearers. Some of our friends trapped, and they taught us how to set traps and skin the animals. The fur from a muskrat skin brought around $1.50, big money for a farm kid in the late '30s and early '40s. We read everything we could about trapping and subscribed to *Fur, Fish and Game Magazine*, which specialized in trapping articles. We spent many Sunday afternoons walking along the banks of the big ditch watching muskrats, learning their habits, and the location of their den entrances.

We purchased a dozen traps, and when the season opened in late November, Dad gave us part of a day off from work to set the traps. I awaited the first morning with great anticipation, dreaming of getting rich from the furs. I had hardly slept that night and awoke before the alarm went off at 4 A.M. We jumped into our clothes, grabbed our flashlights, and pulled on knee boots so we could wade in the water. I was sure the first trap would hold a muskrat, but it was empty, as was the next and the next. We found two snapped traps but never caught one muskrat. Disappointment was written all over our faces as we trudged home. Mother tried to encourage us. "Oh, you will catch one tomorrow."

Dad was glad to see us back by 5:30 A.M. to help with the feeding and milking. He had given us permission to trap with the understanding that we would be back in time to do our chores.

The next morning we again checked our traps in the dark with flashlights. The first few sets were empty, but the fourth one held a nice big muskrat. Our hopes rose, and when we found another in the last trap we were elated. Our dreams of getting rich from the fur business returned.

We caught only twelve muskrats the first season, but that was enough to pay for our traps and provide some profit. We still had a lot to learn about trapping. We read extensively on the subject during the course of the year and talked to other trappers.

During the summer I spent many hours along the dredged ditch learning more of the muskrat's habits. I saw where they had climbed up on the bank at night and eaten corn plants, indicating there were many muskrats living in the ditch below the corn. Dad also noticed the missing corn and encouraged us to trap more muskrats.

The next fall we again set our traps and waited with great anticipation. We found three muskrats in the traps the first morning and two more the following day. We were ecstatic! By the end of the season we had captured thirty-six muskrats, three weasels, two opossums, and one skunk. Our profits were growing.

The skunk turned out to be a near disaster. We knew we had one long before we got to the trap. The countryside reeked with the strong odor. The skunk was still alive—and angry. We were at a loss as to how to dispatch it without getting sprayed. Finally I walked back to the house, got the .22 rifle, and shot it. We let it lie until evening before removing it from the trap. We then tied the skunk to a long pole and carried it home, hanging it behind the chicken house. In spite of our best efforts, some of the skunk odor had gotten on our clothes. Mom made us strip and throw the smelly clothes into a tub of water before entering the house. We washed the clothes with soap and baking soda to get rid of the odor. The skunk smell continued to permeate the air. Mom and our sisters didn't appreciate the foul smell when they went to the chicken house to gather eggs. They complained constantly. We took the smelly animal and hung it behind the hog barn for a few days before we skinned it and disposed of the carcass. It was several days before the foul smell was gone. Joel and I decided that skunks were not worth trapping.

Dad wanted us to trap but he made it clear that farm chores came first and trapping had to be on our own time. We got up at 4 A.M. each morning to check the traps with flashlights, then skinned our catch at night after supper by lantern light. Dad gave us permission to use an empty brooder house as a fur room. Bill Graham and a few other friends who trapped often brought their catches over to skin. We took care of the furs while talking about hunting and trapping. It was an enjoyable social time, but during trapping season Joel and I got little sleep.

Sears Roebuck and Company bought furs from enterprising young trappers in those days and printed a small publication called *Tips to Trappers*, which we ordered and read each year. It had tips on how to catch various fur-bearers and how to skin and preserve the furs. It also listed the dollar values of the various grades of furs. Sears paid premium prices for good, large skins, but less than local buyers for average skins. That second year Joel and I picked out our ten best muskrat furs and sent them to Sears. A few weeks later we received a check for $30. That was a *lot* of money. We didn't tell the local buyer we had sold the top skins to Sears. He paid us the usual $1.50 each for the rest of the muskrats. Our total take for the thirty-six muskrats was nearly $70. We each bought a new bicycle with part of our trapping money.

The next year we expanded our efforts. We bought another dozen traps and got permission from Charley Conwell to trap his part of the ditch. "Boys, dere eatin' my corn," he told us in his thick accent. And they were. They ruined the first four to six rows of his corn growing next to the ditch.

Joel and I were learning a little about conservation, too. We made sure there were plenty of muskrats left at the end of each season. The third year we caught seventy-five muskrats, plus a few weasels and opossums. Charley was happy that we were catching all those 'rats that were eating his corn. We took the praise but failed to inform him that we purposely left plenty each fall for seed the next year.

We gradually honed our techniques of trapping until we were very efficient at taking muskrats and properly preparing the skins. We received premium prices for our furs. Eventually we built up the population and by the early 1940s were harvesting 100 to 150 muskrats each year, earning $200 to $300 for our efforts. That was big money for farm boys in those days, as many farm laborers earned less than five dollars a day. Our parents encouraged our efforts because we were learning to earn money and save it as well.

In 1943, Joel worked on another farm and left the trapping to me. My interest in hunting and trapping grew. I looked forward to the season openings each fall. Trapping put money in my pocket, and hunting put meat on the family table. These activities also increased my knowledge and interest in nature as I diligently studied the animals I hunted and trapped.

Will Troyer with a morning's catch of muskrats from the big dredged ditch

27

A CLASH OF GENERATIONS

Though my parents left the Amish Church in 1934, my father continued to follow many of the conservative Amish rules and customs and tried to impose them on us children as well. He restricted our activities in school and did not permit us to participate in most school sports. He forbade a radio in the house. We kids later defied this order and secretly kept a radio upstairs in one of our bedrooms. He believed that any money we kids earned from outside sources should be split between the child earner and the parents. He was strongly opposed to higher education and let it be known that we children would not be permitted to finish high school.

The latter edict was the hardest for us to accept. We belonged to the Mennonite Church and supposedly were guided by their beliefs and teachings. The Mennonites supported higher education and operated several church colleges in the United States. Nearly all our Mennonite friends planned to finish high school, being encouraged to do so by their parents.

Our father had dropped out of school after the fifth grade and thought this was an adequate education for a farmer. He saw no need for any courses beyond reading, writing, and arithmetic. Mother had completed the eighth grade in the public school system, receiving a diploma for her achievement. As she was quite proud of the diploma, I sensed she did not share my father's firm conviction against a high school education, although she publicly supported his viewpoint. Dad often referred to Mother as being highly educated. He lectured us on the evils of attending school beyond the eighth grade. I suspect he felt a high school or college environment might tempt us to pursue careers other than farming and also lead us to challenge his conservative principles. He was correct in these assumptions.

My brothers, sisters, and I, all good students, wanted to complete high school with our friends who planned on graduating. Very few Indiana farm kids dropped out of school in the 1930s and 1940s. Those that did were usually poor students.

By Indiana law all children had to attend school until age sixteen. The issue of completing high school therefore never really arose until my older sister Almeda turned sixteen.

Almeda had decided on a career in nursing and knew she needed a high school diploma in order to be accepted into a nursing program. She had firm plans for a career, wanting to enter the Mennonite School of Nursing in La Junta, Colorado. She broached the subject of completing high school several times with my parents after her sixteenth birthday, but each time our father gave a firm "No!" to her request. These conversations usually ended with Almeda in tears, but Dad would not relent. I sympathized with my sister and resented my dad as I saw how determined he was to destroy her dreams. I felt helpless to intervene.

Almeda struggled with how to change Dad's unyielding objection to high school. The cause seemed hopeless as our father stubbornly stuck to his viewpoints. She therefore changed tactics, pleading with Mother to intercede on her behalf. Mother had said little on the subject, and we all sensed that she wasn't as adamantly opposed to high school as our father was.

Almeda finally convinced Mother to take up her cause. Cleverly manipulating Dad, Mother argued that becoming a nurse was almost like being a missionary. A nurse administered to other people's needs, and Almeda's desire to become a nurse was paramount to a calling from God. To refuse Almeda to follow this calling was going against the teachings of the Bible. Mother could be quite persuasive when she believed in a cause, and Dad capitulated. He emphasized, however, that he would make this exception only once; the rest of us kids would not be going through high school.

His adamant objections made me more determined than ever to finish high school, but I kept that determination to myself. I saw no need to defy my father so long as an Indiana law kept me in school.

Dad didn't relent on his other stern policies. When I entered high school, I wanted to play basketball. I was a good player and the coach encouraged me to try out for the team. Dad, however, said no to my request, and Mother backed him on this decision. This was difficult for me to accept, as most of my school buddies played on the team. In addition, most of my friends in the Mennonite Church had their parents' permission to play on school teams. I therefore knew the church did not object to the sport, but my parents made it sound like it was religiously wrong to participate in school basketball. I became more resentful toward them.

Dad did give me permission to play baseball one fall. I was surprised. Our school played only three or four other teams during the fall, so the few after-school games didn't take much time away from farm chores. Dad had played baseball as an Amish lad, so perhaps he justified the game on that basis. Regardless, I was appreciative of the small favor. He never relented on the no-basketball rule, however, and I decided not to challenge him on this one. Secretly, I compromised; I would abandon the fight to play basketball but vowed never to yield on my determination to finish high school.

My classmates in school were my best friends and I wanted to complete my education at Clay Township High School with them. I pledged secretly to leave home to finish high school if necessary. I had no firm plans on where I would go.

When my older brother Joel turned sixteen, the high school question again came up. Joel wanted to finish school, but Dad again firmly stood his ground. Joel was an excellent student, but he also tended to be a more obedient son than I. He decided not to fight our father's wishes. He dropped out of school at the end of his sophomore year. I would be next.

I churned inside thinking about the conflict that was coming. About this time I became exceptionally close with my two younger sisters, Sylvia and Miriam. We had adjoining bedrooms upstairs, and we often got together in the evenings to discuss our future. The three of us agreed that as soon as we turned eighteen and were no longer under the legal hand of our parents, we would refuse to bow to their strict rules. Just talking about our mutual problems relieved some of our frustrations.

Sylvia was more defiant than I was in many ways. Once she had gotten into a big argument with our father. He had told her "Shut up!" She refused to be silenced. The confrontation, which started upstairs, turned physical. He pulled her down the stairs one step at a time and slapped her across the face every time she opened her mouth. Still she continued to speak back. By the time they reached the bottom of the stairs, Dad knew he had one defiant daughter. He stomped outside and gave up attempting to physically discipline her any further.

My younger sisters counted on me to break the no-high-school rule. If I failed, their chances of getting the restriction lifted for themselves were nil. I was determined to succeed.

Almeda graduated from high school in 1940. She needed a job to earn money for her nursing school tuition. As I recall, she had to save a minimum of $300, but there weren't many jobs for teenage girls in 1940. She eventually landed a position as a housemaid for a family in Kokomo, receiving $5 a week plus room and board. She came home on weekends. Again, my father's old Amish beliefs created another dilemma for Almeda. Dad ruled that half of the money she earned must be turned over to him until she was twenty-one. This left her with $2.50 per week, and out of these funds she had to buy her own clothes. Although Almeda was very thrifty, it would have taken her years to save enough money for nursing school.

Again Almeda pleaded for Mother to intervene. Mother convinced Dad that since Almeda was answering a religious calling in becoming a nurse, it was only appropriate that they help her financially. Dad again relented, and thereafter Almeda kept her $5-a-week earnings. She worked two years to save enough money to enter nurse's training in Colorado.

I think it was easier for Dad to make exceptions for Almeda than for a defiant child like Sylvia or me. Almeda was rather quiet, a model daughter who rarely did anything wrong. She was the oldest and took her responsibilities seriously. She had big soft eyes that tended to break down a stern father's rules without lifting her voice. We younger kids were happy to see her get a few special privileges, since we felt she deserved them. I also secretly intended to get those exceptions from my dad, but I knew they would come at the cost of a big fight.

When I turned sixteen and was in my sophomore year in high school, the big confrontation finally came. We were eating supper and Sylvia made some innocent remark about my continuing through school. Dad stopped eating and laid his fork down.

"I didn't know Willard vas gonna go to high school next year," he said.

I immediately replied in a very firm, loud voice. "I am going through high school! If you try to stop me, I'll leave home!"

Suddenly, everyone stopped eating and there was absolute silence. I had made the statement in such an unwavering voice that my father knew I intended to carry out the threat. For a full minute not a word was spoken as I glared at my dad. Everyone else looked down at his plate. I had laid down the challenge, and my brothers and sisters now wondered what Dad was going to do. He didn't speak but looked at me with hurt eyes for a few moments, then he placed his elbows on the table, cradled his face in his hands and wept. He had done this before to get his way on some deeply contested issue. Perhaps he thought this tactic would change my mind, but it had the opposite effect. I believed in the old adage "Grown men don't cry." His act diminished my respect for my dad. We bolted down our food and left the table until only Mom and Dad remained. I have no idea what was said between them.

My father and I didn't speak to each other for days after the confrontation, and the rift between us only deepened. He never again ordered me to drop out of high school.

Many of my teachers and friends at school had encouraged me to finish high school but wondered if I would be able to overcome my father's objections. They knew Dad had prevented Joel from continuing. I never informed them of the fight I'd had at home and I never gloated over winning the battle. I simply kept my feelings bottled up inside me. My only release was when I discussed them with my sisters. They were relieved that I had challenged Dad and won. He didn't try to stop my younger siblings from completing high school, and all of them graduated.

At age sixteen I still had not decided to go to college, but I knew I wanted to have a career with more adventure than farming offered. I continued to read extensively on natural history and had decided to become a naturalist, but I had no idea how you entered such a field. One of my teachers, Mrs. Underwood, encouraged me to dream big and pointed out various books that might interest me. Almeda continued to bring home travel and nature books from the Kokomo Library each weekend. I read incessantly of Martin and Osa Johnson's adventures in Africa while they photographed wildlife. I devoured the books of Frank Buck of "Bring 'em Back Alive" fame. He spent years capturing exotic wildlife in remote regions of the world and sold them to zoos in the United States. I explored the world with Theodore Roosevelt and Roy Chapman Andrews and many other adventurers. I studied the nature writings of Ernest Thompson Seton, Enos Mills, John James Audubon, and John Muir. Mrs. Underwood read some of these books, primarily I think, so that she could discuss them with me. She certainly had a beneficial influence on my life during this critical time of my youth.

I graduated from high school in 1944. My father never really relented from his objections to higher education. He didn't come to my graduation or to any of my other school events, but Mother did. After Dad and I had our big confrontation on the subject of high school, he never brought up the subject again but I don't think he ever changed his mind. He just accepted the inevitable, reluctantly. The barrier between us softened only slightly as time passed. He had seen my wandering ways and thought he could change me if he kept me away from the influences of high school.

Our parents had brought us into a different culture, however, when they took us out of the Amish society and into the more liberal Mennonite Church—and into a different public school system with no other Mennonite or Amish students. My father still clung to many of his old beliefs, which we as a younger generation could not accept, so it was inevitable that there would be a clash.

Years later I finally was able to look objectively at my father's background and understand why he opposed so many of my dreams and desires. It was a long time before I lost the bitterness that developed between us and was able to forgive him for those actions that caused me so much trauma in my youth.

28

BICYCLE WEST

The Hartman boys and I often talked about taking a bicycle trip to Texas, to visit their two uncles who were cattle ranchers in the state. We thought it would be a great adventure and figured the round trip would take about a month. We planned the journey for several summers, but each year it got delayed because our parents couldn't spare us from the farm work. Fate intervened the summer after I finished high school.

One afternoon while hauling bundles during the July threshing season, I noticed there were only six shocks of wheat left in the field. I decided to add them to my already full load. The extra shocks made the load extremely high and a little top-heavy. I started toward the barn proudly driving the biggest load of the season, when the wagon's left front wheel dropped into a rut. The wagon tipped and sent me flying through the air. I landed on my head and right shoulder, stunned for a moment as a dagger of pain shot through my shoulder. Leonard Hartman stopped his team and came running over. "Are ya hurt?"

I answered with a moan and contorted grimace as I slowly staggered to my feet. The excruciating pain in my shoulder continued to throb. I slowly walked back to the house while Leonard took care of my horses and the upset bundle wagon. Mother examined me briefly, rubbed some liniment on my shoulder and told me to lie down and rest. She thought I had sprained my arm and shoulder and assumed it would heal in a few days. But the pain continued, and I was unable to raise my right arm. A few days later Mother took me to our family doctor, who advised me to see a chiropractor.

The chiropractor diagnosed the problem as a dislocated clavicle; he said he could correct it. I lay on my stomach while the chiropractor gently put one hand on my shoulder and firmly grasped my right arm.

"Now this won't hurt," he assured me.

I relaxed at those soothing words as he gave my arm and shoulder a firm snap. "Ouch!" I yelled and writhed in pain, nearly passing out. Beads of sweat rolled down my face. He then explained that my bones were back in place, but I would not be able to work on the farm for several weeks while I recovered.

I felt better in a few days but was unable to raise my right arm over my shoulder without extreme pain; therefore, I couldn't do much farm work.

Then the thought struck me. If I could ride a bicycle, I could take that long-awaited trip while I was convalescing! Since I wasn't able to work, my parents shouldn't object to my leaving. I got on the bicycle, leaned forward, resting my arms on the handlebars, and rode down the lane. No pain!

I eagerly planned the trip. Since I was going alone, I decided to head for Yellowstone National Park rather than Texas. I thought the Rocky Mountains would be much more interesting to explore. I wasn't sure I could pedal all the way to Yellowstone, so I decided not to tell anyone of my destination in case I failed.

That evening I told Mom and Dad of my plans. I argued that since I was unable to do any heavy farm work, now would be a good time for me to take a short bicycle trip. They weren't too enthusiastic about such an adventure in my physical condition, but they didn't have any good objections. I informed them I would be traveling to Illinois, perhaps Iowa, and would be gone at least a week. I'm sure Mother had some trepidation about my leaving on a bicycle trip with an injured shoulder, but she hid her feelings and wished me well.

The next morning I left on my single-speed balloon-tired bicycle. It was equipped with a front basket and a rear carrier with saddlebags. Having no previous experience in long bicycle trips, I decided to carry a minimum amount of equipment. I packed a sweater, an extra shirt, socks, underwear, a canteen of water, and a sleeping bag. I had no raincoat or tent and my only cooking utensils were a fork, a spoon, and a bowl. I planned on eating groceries that didn't require cooking and on buying an occasional restaurant meal. I also carried a pocketknife, a few tools, and $80 in cash.

As I pedaled down the farm lane, waving goodbye to my family, I had some qualms. Could I really bike all the way to Yellowstone National Park? I had been out of Indiana only once, and that was to Kentucky. I had no conception of what it would be like to travel across the western prairies and mountains. Did I have the physical stamina to cross the mountains on a bike? How long would it really take? These thoughts raced through my mind as my home disappeared from view. I had many doubts and fears but I was exhilarated, thinking about the trip ahead.

I pedaled furiously leaving the graveled country roads behind. Biking was much easier on the paved state road and the miles sped by. My legs were strong and I was averaging better than 10 mph. By early afternoon I had pedaled sixty miles and toward evening I crossed into Illinois. I was elated, for just getting to another state was a major achievement in my mind. By the time the sun set in the west, I had been riding nearly twelve hours and had traveled over a hundred miles. I was satisfied with my first day's effort, so I stopped and pushed the bike into a tall cornfield. I rolled out the sleeping bag and went to sleep to the night chorus of crickets.

In the morning my leg muscles were a bit stiff from the previous day's ride, but as I rode west I soon forgot about my sore legs. I stopped at a small grocery store and bought a quart of milk and a package of cinnamon rolls for breakfast.

I made good time traveling across the flat Illinois countryside. Two days later I crossed the Mississippi River and entered the rolling hills of Iowa. I struggled to pedal up the numerous hills but enjoyed the downhill stretches. I also bucked westerly winds, which slowed my efforts. Hour after hour went by and one day flowed into another. It was rather monotonous with field after field of corn. I stopped to chat with farmers who were cultivating corn just as I did in Indiana. It seemed I would never get away from cornfields, but I kept those bicycle wheels turning.

Several days later I crossed the Nebraska border, and then I was biking through the wide-open spaces of the Nebraska Sandhills. This hay and cattle country was quite different from the Midwestern corn belt and I was excited to finally see a change from the landscape I had known all my life. It was hot. Several times a day I stopped at ranch houses with windmills to get a cool drink and replenish the water in my canteen. The owners usually wanted to know where I had come from and where I was going. By then I was convinced I would succeed in reaching Yellowstone Park and I informed them of my destination. Their eyes lit up, "Golly! You gonna pedal all that way! I hope you make it."

The Nebraska ranchers were friendly people and I think they enjoyed my stopping for a drink of water as much as I did.

The open prairies provided few hiding places where I could sleep at night and not be seen from the road. Usually I rolled out my sleeping bag behind a haystack or in a deep gully, but one evening I could find no visible cover until I passed a culvert under a railroad track that paralleled the road. I figured that should be a good place to sleep.

I hid the bike on the other side of the track and rolled out the sleeping bag in the three-foot-diameter culvert. A loud noise startled me awake about 2 A.M. and I smacked my head on the culvert before I realized a train was passing overhead. The train wheels, only a few feet above my head, made one awful racket. I stuck my fingers in my ears until the long train passed. I resumed my sleep, but it was the last time I slept in a train culvert.

I had never seen mountains, but I had read John Muir's vivid description of mountain landscapes and I was getting anxious to experience them. The Rocky Mountains were still many days away, so I turned north in western Nebraska and headed for the Black Hills of South Dakota. As I approached the foothills, the mountain features became more pronounced. Hour after hour I rode toward the distant peaks, but the closer I got, the harder I had to pedal. Soon I was struggling to maintain even a slow speed. After a few miles of intense physical effort, I was convinced there was something wrong with the bike. I pulled off the road, turned the bicycle upside down and spun the wheels. Everything seemed in working order, which perplexed me. Then, as I mounted the bicycle again, I looked back down the road and noticed the steep incline.

This was my first time traveling in mountains, so I didn't know about the illusion of appearing to travel on level terrain while in reality going uphill. With a one-speed bike I was unable to gear down, so I just had to increase my effort. I finally got to Custer, South Dakota, and decided I'd had enough mountain biking for a while and turned west toward Wyoming. The highway out of Custer had a gradual downhill slope, and I now reaped the benefits of my uphill struggle. I raced down the relatively straight highway. The bicycle didn't have a speedometer, but I knew I could pedal 35 mph and I surpassed that speed by far. I leaned over the handlebars and listened to the tires zing and the wind whistle past my ears. I estimated my speed at 50 mph when I rounded a slight curve and noticed a truck just ahead. I rapidly gained on the vehicle and moved into the left lane. As I whizzed past the truck, I glimpsed an old rancher in a big cowboy hat suddenly snap to attention.

I wondered what his thoughts were as I sped past his old truck.

A day or so later near Gillette, Wyoming, I found myself in the real wild west that I had so often dreamed about. The country had wide-open spaces with real cowboys on horses herding cattle. Antelope and a few mule deer grazed on the range. I was fascinated by it all. The Bighorn Mountains of Wyoming loomed in the distance. I was to discover that crossing them would be a major obstacle on my way to Yellowstone National Park.

On a Sunday evening near Sheridan, Wyoming, I approached the bottom of a steep pass that led over the Bighorns. I stopped and ate a large dinner, knowing there would be some heavy biking ahead. The incline eventually became too steep to bike, so I got off and started pushing the bicycle. The drivers of several cars stopped to ask my destination. When I informed them it was Yellowstone Park, they usually shook their head in disbelief. One driver informed me it was impossible to cross the mountains by bicycle and urged me to turn back. Then he inquired, "Where ya from?" When I told him, he exploded, "Ye gods, maybe you *will* make it!"

I trudged on and late in the evening a flat-bottomed ravine in a pine forest presented itself. I pulled off, rolled out my sleeping bag, and slept soundly. Sometime during the night a porcupine chewed my leather belt in two. I had lost considerable weight and my pants wouldn't stay up. I solved the problem by inserting a piece of baling wire I found through the trouser loops. It sufficed until I got to the next town and bought a new belt.

I walked and pushed the bike several more miles before reaching the summit. Now, I thought, it would be all downhill. An inexperienced mountain traveler, I learned I had to travel sixty miles across the Bighorns before I could descend the other side. World War II was in progress; there were few travelers and hence few tourist facilities open. I became quite hungry, as I hadn't eaten since I started up the mountains the evening before. About mid-afternoon I found an open gas station that carried a few candy bars. The sweets relieved my hunger for a while.

That afternoon I met a sheepherder tending his flock. He warned me that the road down the mountain was extremely steep with hairpin curves. He knew of only one other biker who had attempted the descent, and he had burned out his brakes and crashed. I thanked him for the information.

Late in the afternoon I started down the steep mountain road, riding the brakes constantly to slow my speed and maneuver around dangerous hairpin curves. I began to smell something hot, like burning rubber, and recalled the sheepherder's warning. I stopped and checked the brakes, which were too hot to touch! Thereafter, I would ride a short distance, stopping at each ravine where streams tumbled down the mountain to pour cool water on the brakes. I finally made it to the bottom unscathed, thankful for the sheepherder's warning.

The Rocky Mountains now loomed ahead, their crests disappearing into the high clouds. It was a grand scene, and this Indiana farm boy gazed in wonder. Awed and excited by the immensity of the mountains, I realized I would accomplish my goal of reaching Yellowstone National Park.

Thirteen days and 1550 miles after leaving Indiana I entered the eastern entrance to the park. The ranger at the gate seemed astounded when I informed him of my long journey. He gave me a free pass and warned me about bears. It was late in the evening and became dark before I reached the first campground. I pulled off the road and spent an uncomfortable night trying to sleep in a steep rocky ravine.

The next day I bought a postcard and sent it to my parents. I was proud that I had achieved my goal but knew I must have caused my parents some anxiety when I didn't return at the end of the first week.

It was in the park that I became aware I could again raise my right arm high enough to comb my hair. My injured shoulder was healing despite all the physical strain of biking.

I spent three days in Yellowstone, mostly around Old Faithful. During that time I had my first adventure with a black bear. I had left some cookies in the saddlebags. During the night a bear stole the cookies and knocked over the bicycle. Awakened by the noise, I screamed at the bear and fortunately it left. That would be a good story to tell my buddies back in Indiana. I also got caught in a hailstorm, which I weathered by standing under a tree with the sleeping bag draped over my head. The padded bag protected me from the cherry-sized hailstones that pounded through the tree for twenty minutes.

Will Troyer just before entering Yellowstone National Park on his bicycle trip

I left Yellowstone via the West Gate, then headed south through Idaho, toward Salt Lake City. It was in Idaho that I biked 156 miles in one day, the record for the trip. In Salt Lake I turned east, planning to visit my sister Almeda in La Junta, Colorado, where she was completing her nurse's training.

Between Salt Lake City and Grand Junction, Colorado, I encountered some of the most difficult times on the entire trip. It was August, extremely hot, and I often had a problem finding water in the hot desert country. I learned to carry oranges to quench my thirst and supplement the small canteen of water. Sometimes I traveled at night, when it was cooler. Eventually I made it across this dry, hot stretch of country and entered the mountains of Colorado.

Several days later near Gunnison, Colorado, I became ill. I was nauseated and weak with a fever. Worst of all, I was approaching the 11,000-foot Monarch Pass and knew I had to be in good physical condition to cross those high mountains. I rested a day and toward evening the fever subsided. A trucker stopped and asked me if I would assist him in loading his truck with peaches in exchange for a ride across the mountains. I looked at the high peaks and, in my weakened condition, I accepted the offer.

The next day we loaded the truck with peaches and started the long, slow grind over the Rockies. Sometime during the following night we passed La Junta, where my sister lived. I decided not to abandon the free lift and to ride the peach truck all the way to the Kansas border. This took a few days as the trucker had girlfriends in several towns and stopped each night for romantic visits. The 400-mile ride took three days to complete but saved me at least five days of hard biking. I had filled my stomach with peaches and was in top physical condition again.

After helping the trucker unload the peaches, I resumed my bike journey. A day later I discovered my tires were worn quite thin. Sand burrs, which were common in western Kansas, were able to puncture the tires. I needed new tires and purchased a set with my meager cash reserves. I now had only $12 left to complete the journey. I cut back on food to save money. A week later I crossed the Indiana border, lustily singing "Back Home Again in Indiana."

On a Sunday afternoon I rode up to George Ehrman's house to announce I was back. I had been gone forty days and biked about four thousand miles, quite an achievement for a young farm lad. George Ehrman, typically enthusiastic, phoned my parents and other friends to inform them that I had safely returned and was sitting in his house. Friends gathered to hear of my adventures. It was a hot day, and I had arrived at the Ehrmans shirtless. I had lost twenty-eight pounds and some of my friends simply stared at my skinny body. My mother was particularly proud that I had traveled farther by bicycle than she ever had by train or car. She had always wanted to take a trip out west but never had the opportunity, so she was full of questions about my adventures.

That evening a local newspaper reporter called me for an interview; George Ehrman had informed him of my trip. The following day a short story about my biking adventures appeared on the front page of the Kokomo Tribune. I was now a local hero. Many friends, including the Hartman boys, envied me and wished they had accompanied me on the trip. Rumors spread that I had biked all the way to the Pacific Coast and back, which I had to set straight. Even Dad gloated a bit to his friends that his adventurous son had taken the trip of a lifetime.

My shoulder had completely healed, so I was soon busy on the farm helping with the fall harvest. I was glad to be back in some ways, but I kept thinking about the wide-open spaces I had seen and the high mountains I had crossed. I had tasted adventure and knew that someday I would return to the mountains of the west.

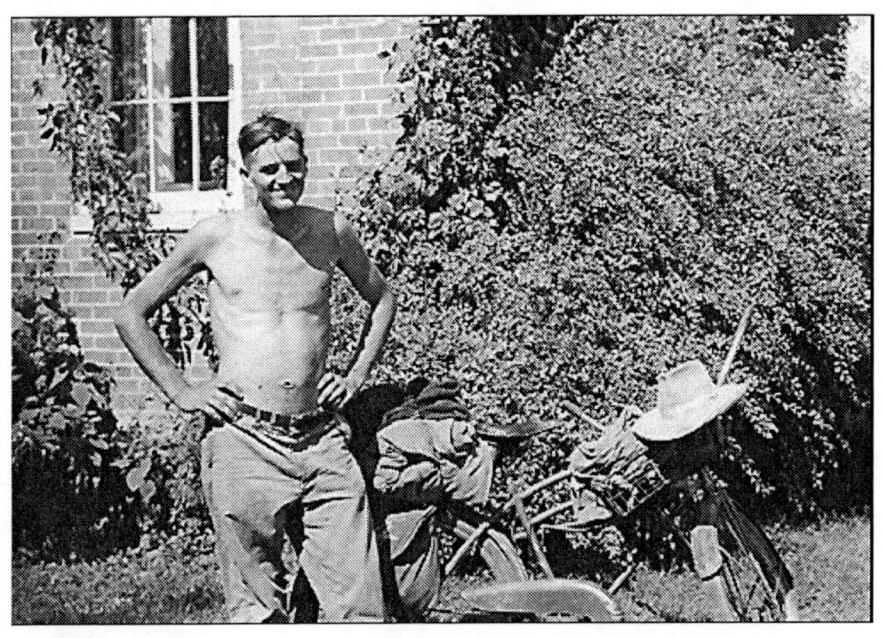

The day I returned from my 4000-mile bicycle trip to Yellowstone. I had lost 28 pounds.

29

FAREWELL TO THE FARM

I had often dreamed of leaving the farm, but when the time came I found it hard to do. I was a product of the farm environment; many aspects of farm life were gratifying to me. I loved spring when the crops were planted and the newborn lambs, pigs, calves, and chicks arrived. I cherished the smell of fruit blossoms and a clover field in bloom. I looked forward to the return of the robins, the warbling bluebirds, the bobolinks, and the singing meadowlarks. I also enjoyed fall when the cellar, grain bins, and corncribs were brimming, full from the harvest. I was exhilarated to watch a team of horses lean into their traces and move a heavy loaded wagon. I liked the neighborhood social life while threshing, making apple butter, and butchering. But in the end I had little choice about leaving.

World War II had been raging since my early teens. In many ways we were immune to the conflicts that seemed so far away but we were also constantly reminded of the war. The Kokomo Tribune kept us informed of the war's progress, the bombing of large cities, the number of planes shot down, ships sunk, the many battles won and lost. Gas, sugar, and tires were rationed, and other shortages were caused by the war. In the skies above our farm, young pilots from a nearby naval air base staged mock aerial battles as they trained for warfare. Everyone had sons or neighbors who were in the armed forces. Patriotism ran high, and many young boys wanted to join the fracas. I was no exception.

By 1945, many of my school buddies had left for the Army, Navy, Marines, and Air Force. I didn't want to be left behind, but there seemed to be plenty of time. The war was expected to last several more years as the Japanese vowed never to surrender. At the request of my dad and Harry Hartman, the local military draft board had granted me an agriculture deferment to help with the farm harvest in 1945. I decided not to seek an extension and to enter the Armed Forces right after the fall harvest. When I informed my parents of my military decision, they were heartbroken. Descendants of a long line of conscientious objectors, they did not believe in participating in war or violence. Non-violence is a basic tenet of both the Mennonite and Amish religions. Many of our ancestors had been killed for refusing to participate in the armed conflicts of Europe. But I was caught up in the patriotic enthusiasm of stopping the Germans and Japanese—and determined to follow my own conscience.

This disagreement with my parents put an additional stress on our already-strained relationship, and we talked very little.

Ever since my parents had lost their first farm during the Depression, they had struggled to save enough money to purchase another one. During the early 1940s prices for agriculture products gradually increased, and by the fall of 1945, some fourteen years after my parents lost the McGrawsville farm, they had saved enough money to make a substantial down payment on another farm. Because land prices were cheaper in northern Indiana, they purchased a 160-acre farm near Goshen, Indiana, and planned to move that winter. My younger brothers, Omar and Philip, were now old enough to help with the chores and fieldwork. It was a good time for me to leave the farm.

Then the atomic bomb was dropped on Japan; a few weeks later, the war was over. I was concerned I might not be called after all. It became apparent, however, that young men were needed to replace those who had been in the conflict for many years and wanted to return home.

I received orders for induction into the Army a few months later. As I left the farm and headed for the induction center in Indianapolis, I knew my life was about to undergo a drastic change. I drove past the fields where I had toiled for so many years and watched the familiar barns and old farmhouses fade in the distance. I sped by the Conwell, Graham, and Hartman farms and the Clay Howard School. This small section of Indiana was my entire life. I wondered if I would return. The thought caused a big lump in my throat and I bit my lips to fight back tears.

During my short military service I met young men from many parts of the United States with a variety of backgrounds. That experience broadened my perspective of the careers available. Some of my Army buddies wanted to become truck drivers, factory workers, carpenters, or to return to the farm. Others, however, planned to attend college under the G. I. Bill that was available to ex-servicemen. They wanted to become doctors, lawyers, teachers, engineers, or other professionals. I too began to consider college as an option.

After serving less than two years in the Army, I was discharged and now had to make a decision on a profession. I was still interested in nature and wildlife, but I didn't know how to make this a paying career. Then one day I remembered a meeting our high school class had had with one of our teachers. He was discussing careers and asked each of us about our future plans. We were all farm kids and many of my classmates indicated they wanted to remain on the farm. When it came my turn I said something about wildlife, in a barely audible voice, as I felt a little embarrassed to be different. The teacher's eyes lit up. "Now, Willard, if you're interested in a career in wildlife, you should write to the Department of the Interior in Washington, D.C. and request a list of the colleges that teach wildlife biology."

At the time I wasn't considering college seriously, but I must have tucked that bit of information in the back of my mind. Soon after being discharged, I wrote for a list of colleges that taught wildlife. A year later I entered a small college near my parents' new farm in northern Indiana. On weekends I went home and helped with the farming. My intentions were to take the basic courses required in Indiana, then transfer to Michigan State College, where they offered a degree in wildlife biology. But I couldn't get the West that I had seen on my bicycle trip out of my mind.

The next year I enrolled in the Wildlife Department at Oregon State College in Corvallis, Oregon. I became friends with many enthusiastic students who were studying for a career in wildlife management.

I graduated from college in 1952 and immediately was employed by the U.S. Fish and Wildlife Service in Alaska. It was a dream come true for a farm boy from Indiana who had always been interested in nature. I spent my entire career in Alaska, studying and managing various species of wildlife and having adventures that I had so often read and dreamed about in my youth.

Farming still grips me, however. Each spring I get the urge to plant a garden in the north country and watch it grow. In the summer and the fall, when I fill the freezer with salmon, grouse, moose, or deer and pick a supply of wild berries, I get the same satisfaction that I did in filling the grain bins and the root cellar on the farm.

During my career in Alaska I returned to Indiana many times and gradually saw farming practices and lifestyles change. Soon after World War II everything became mechanized, and horses disappeared from the farm. The tractors and other equipment got bigger. The old, small, outdated equipment that we used on the farm now sat rusting in the many implement graveyards. The bigger equipment cost a lot of money, and a 160-acre farm was no longer capable of supporting a family. It now took three to four hundred acres. Ten-acre fields became a nuisance for farmers with the big equipment, so many of the fences were removed.

Other farming practices also changed. Pesticides and herbicides never used before were now applied to eliminate weeds and insects. The small family herds of dairy cows and feeder cattle became things of the past. If you didn't have cattle, there was no need to raise clover or alfalfa, so the practice of crop rotation stopped. Farmers now saturated the fields with commercial fertilizers to replace the manure the livestock had provided. Farm country became one of corn and soybeans. A large number of cattle and hogs were now fed in huge feed lots, and the manure often became a pollution problem rather than an asset. Many of the small wood lots were cut down because they were no longer needed to graze small numbers of cattle and hogs and produce wood for the family stoves. City people wanted a house in the woods, so many former wood lots became subdivisions as city residents moved to the countryside. In just a few decades the farm country of my youth was drastically changed.

A few years ago I had an urge to again hear the call of a bobwhite quail, warbling bluebirds, and the songs of the bobolinks and meadowlarks. I returned to the land of my youth in the late spring, but no bobwhites called, because the fencerows that served as nesting habitat had been removed. I heard no bobolinks because there were no clover fields. I failed to hear the song of the bluebird or meadowlark; I suspect many had been killed by pesticides.

The next day I walked through the nearby Francis Slocum State Recreation area. The land surrounding the river reservoir is managed by the Indiana Department of Conservation. Former farm fields have been permitted to revert back to brush, weeds, and grasslands. The department has also planted small plots of grain for wildlife. I heard bluebirds warbling and saw an abundance of meadowlarks, brown thrashers, goldfinch, warblers, and other birds I had known in my youth. It was obvious that where there is good habitat, wildlife thrives.

In late July, I drove across northern Indiana through the heart of Amish country. I saw Amish farmers tilling their fields with horses. Shocked fields of oats and wheat dotted the landscape. I watched several Amish boys hauling grain bundles to a threshing machine near a big hip-roofed barn. This was the farming country of my youth, with a mixture of corn, wheat, oats, and clover fields. Dairy cows grazed in the pastures and the barn lots were filled with hogs and chickens. These small farms still supply the needs of an Amish family because they thrive on old-fashioned values and a simple lifestyle. They don't need to spend thousands of dollars to buy huge tractors and combines. They survive without cars, electricity, and central heating.

It was a nostalgic journey for me. They say you can't go back because everything changes. Perhaps that's true, but that day I was again reminded of those old-fashioned values of honesty, simplicity, and hard work. I was also reminded of the close-knit social life that has shaped my life and that of many other generations of this nation. Yes, modern technology has made life much easier physically, but were the losses of these values worth the gain of the fast and easy life? It is something to think about.

LaVergne, TN USA
15 December 2009
167152LV00003B/56/A